Money Sense for Young Professionals

Save More for Life's Priorities

WILLIAM STANLEY

Your very own Money Coach

PAGE PUBLISHING, INC.
New York, NY

First originally published by Page Publishing, Inc. 2019

Photo Attribution—Tim Bresnahan, Tim Bresnahan Photo

ISBN 978-1-64544-940-9 (Paperback)
ISBN 978-1-64544-941-6 (Digital)

Printed in the United States of America

CONTENTS

You, the Young Professional

How Is Your Generation Different and Why?

The following are the generations:

- ☐ Silent generation: born 1928–1945 (74-91 years old as of 2019)
- ☐ Baby boomer: born 1946–1964 (55-72 years old as of 2019)
- ☐ Generation X: born 1965–1980 (39-54 years old as of 2019); also includes Xennials (born 1975+)
- ☐ Millennial: born 1981–1996 (23-38 years old as of 2019); also includes Generation Y or Generation Next (born 1980+) and iGen or Generation Z (born 1995+)
- ☐ Postmillennial: born 1997–present

Each generation grows up in their own unique times, yet we have more in common than generally thought. The following highlight some of the differences and some of the commonalities between generations.

How to Attract Millennials

Each generation is different, including millennials; disconnect from previous generations is not new. We are a "learn how to learn" generation. Our obsession is learning: "Tell me your story. Let's do it together." We search for meaning and expect quick results. We will quit our jobs quickly if we don't make a difference in six months.

"Personally, home ownership is not on my list. We live with her parents, and I am proud we were able to pay off $20,000 in student debt in ten months." Building wealth is important but for different reasons. It is all about community.

> (Tyler Hill, millennial, cofounder of local coffee
> shop, hospitality consultant, September 2018)

Millennials: Myth and Reality

<u>Myth</u>: Millennials don't want to invest in the stock market.

Reality: They understand equity risk.

<u>Myth</u>: Millennials only use robo-advisers.

Reality: Many prefer working with a human financial adviser.

<u>Myth</u>: Millennials don't have good money habits.

Reality: Their savings and budgeting efforts match those of other generations.

<u>Myth</u>: Millennials are all the same.

Reality: No generation is homogeneous—especially one this diverse.

<u>Myth</u>: Millennials have no interest in planning for retirement.

Reality: They have competing priorities for their spare dollars.

(From *InvestmentNews*, October 29, 2018.)

The Financial Crisis of 2008 Set Millennials Back— But It May Have Made Them Better with Money

Of those ages sixteen to twenty-five, 81% watched their parents struggle in the Great Recession, and this seems to have a positive influence on millennials when it comes to how they save.

Retirement savings is a higher priority for many millennials, right up there with food and housing. About half with a 401(k) contribute 10% or more.

Older millennials have felt the effects of the Great Recession. The level of wealth in 2016 is 34% below the levels of other generation at that stage in life.

Younger adults say their parents helped them become financially responsible, but safety was overemphasized. As a result, many save rather than invest.

Many millennials remain spooked by the stock market and are reluctant to invest outside of workplace retirement accounts; 20% hold no stocks in retirement accounts. Less than a quarter have IRAs, and only 12% use brokerage accounts.
(From CNBC, September 2018.)

Lehman Anniversary: The Five Most Surprising Consequences

Just 19% of millennials agree with the statement "Generally speaking, most people can be trusted." Compared to 31% for previous generations. Millennials trust Wall Street least of all.
(From BBC, September 2018)

How Millennials Are Reshaping Car Buying

Often saddled with debt, young shoppers are looking for smaller cheaper vehicles and are more likely to do their research online.
(From BBC, September 2018)

Renting Your Place? Skipping This Could Cost You

Millennials are more likely to rent than to own their homes, but nearly six in ten don't have renters' insurance.
(From CNBC, February 2015.)

Millennials Redefine Luxury—and the Stakes Are High

Every generation brings its own trend, its own taste, its own way of living. The younger generation is more disruptive.

According to the U.S. Chamber of Commerce, millennials have about $300 billion in direct purchasing power and account for $500 billion more through parental influence. Aside from being more tech-savvy, millennials are more willing to experiment with emerging brands.

The meaning of "luxury" is changing. It no longer means handbags or jewelry; it now includes farm-to-table foods, craft beers, and pricey experiences, such as travel. Millennials also accept renting instead of owning luxury.

(From CNBC, February 2015.)

Millennial Money Habits Worth Breaking

Overspending, undersaving, and racking up credit card debt are some common offenders among young professionals. Almost four in ten of the millennials surveyed by Fidelity admit to worrying at least once a week about their financial future. The good news is, it may not be as hard to break those bad habits as you think.

They can be fixed through a number of ways:
☐ Track your spending.
☐ Plan ahead for big spending.
☐ Set up an emergency fund.

(From CNBC, February 2015.)

Millennials Set to Be the Fattest Generation

UK millennials are on track to be the most overweight generation since records began, health experts say. Based on population trends, more than seven in every ten people born between the early 1980s and mid 1990s will be too fat by the time they reach middle age.

Money Coach comment: even though this is about the UK, we in the US should know well that being healthy is better than being wealthy.

(From BBC, February 2018.)

The Disconnect between Baby Boomers and Millennials— Work Ethic

Baby boomers often believe millennials are entitled and lazy, but this couldn't be further from the truth. Millennials enter a professional world where reality is wildly different from what boomers knew. Their environment has different demands. Boomers have certain expectations of young employees based on their own experience.

Millennials expect to be fired or let go regularly, so they want their work to be directly in line with their own career equity. They need to feel like what they are working toward aligns with their own goals and aspirations. They worked hard for my company because they felt they were getting something out of it that benefitted them.

There is a way to build mutually beneficial relationship between generations, and it comes from compromise on both sides.

(Quora.com, September 2018.)

Stefanic Casts Net for Millennial-Related Policy Ideas

Only 24% of millennials have demonstrated basic financial knowledge. Skyrocketing student debt must be brought under control. Millennials are cynical about the solvency of Social Security.

(From Elise Stefanik, congressional
committee focusing on millennials.)

PROLOGUE 2

Me, Your Money Coach

I am not your generation; I prefer to call myself Generation S (seniors) or Generation E (experience). My generation has many "perennials"—we keep blooming year after year.

How do I know your generation? I've raised three kids, now in their thirties and early forties. I have four grandkids; I know the importance of early education when it comes to money. I work closely with elementary and high school kids as well as young adults. I have interviewed scores of Young Professionals for this book. I want you to learn from them—what they have done right and what mistakes they have made. Many of their comments are included in this book. Learn from your peers. If they can be successful, so can you.

Financial Literacy is my goal. You don't often find it in school. You may have grown up in a family where money was a continuing problem. It is time to learn from your Money Coach.

In this book I also use my own experience. I grew up with frugal parents and learned to carefully manage what little money I had. When something broke, my family would fix it, not buy something new. My mother encouraged my sister and me to save money whenever we could. My father cautioned us never to buy anything unless we first had saved the money. I have always handled my own money and, in the 1980's, I wrote a newsletter, "Money Sense," for family and friends. I have learned from my many money mistakes. Mistakes are OK, but you must say to yourself, "I won't do that again."

I have acquired many ideas from my clients over the years—how to do things right and how money mistakes can ruin an otherwise good life.

Life is full of choices. It is up to you to decide when to move in a better direction with your finances. You can begin now, you can begin later, or you can never begin. I want you to choose the right path to financial success. That's why I wrote this book.

CHAPTER 1

Money Basics

Smart Finances for Young Professionals

Listen to Your Mother

Live within Your Means: What Does That Mean?

Financial Goals: The How-To

When You Might Need a Money Coach

Take the Money Coach Test: The Financial Checkup

The Big Money Picture

A Money Exercise for All

Learn from Kids

Smart Finances for Young Professionals

Financial Planning Is Simply Taking Charge of Your Money

You can start now.
You can start later.
You can never start.
The start time is up to you—and only you.

Want to Be a Millionaire?

Start by learning how to spot a millionaire. A millionaire shuts the light off when he/she leaves the room. Be frugal and wise if you want to be a millionaire. Saving a little over a long period will help you tremendously. Start early and keep adding to the account. Start today!

Take Control

Take control of your money no matter how much or how little you have.

Learn as much as you can. Apply that learning.

You've heard of street smarts. Develop "money smarts."

Set goals. Achievable goals for yourself. Short, medium, long term—write them down. Do it now!

It's Not How Much You Make; It's How Much You Spend

You do the best you know how to earn as much as you can based upon your education and your attitude.

You don't have full control over how much you earn.

You do have control over how much you spend.

When you budget, you keep track of where your money goes. That way, you know how much you spend.

What You Want Is Not Always What You Need

This advice is from my stepdaughter, who, in her teens and twenties, was always buying things she later decided she did not need.

Learn from Your Mistakes

This is a lesson in life. Mistakes are okay, but we must reflect upon them and learn not to make the same mistake again. Avoid paying a "service charge" on your bank account or buying something over the phone from an unsolicited phone call, a telemarketer. Just say, "Sorry, I do not accept telephone solicitations." Then hang up.

Write down some money mistakes you have made. Write down mistakes you have made and are not going to make again.

Investing Is Not Gambling

Educate yourself about investing. It is not that hard. You can do it!

Protect Your Health, and Amass a lot of Wealth

Avoid tobacco and alcohol and sugary stuff.

If you now spend $50 per month on beer and cigarettes and instead invest the money at 8% gain compounded annually, you could have nearly $175,000 after forty years.

Despite perceptions that it is healthier, there is little difference between bottled water and tap water per the World Wildlife Fund. Often the only difference between bottled water and tap water is that it is distributed in bottles rather than pipes. Bottled water can cost up to a thousand times more than tap water.

Listen to Your Mother

We honor Mom on her special day each year in May, but we should forever follow Mom's advice on money matters.

"Look both ways before crossing the street." Streets are dangerous; you must be careful. The world of finances is also a dangerous place; people are often trying to take advantage of you. Enter this world with caution, and keep your eyes open. Learn the basics. Question everything.

"Save for a rainy day." This is a very important piece of advice from Mom. It translates to having an emergency fund to pay for unexpected things that might happen. If you have an emergency fund, you don't have to put emergency expenses on a credit card.

"Don't put all your eggs in one basket." This means diversify your investments. Don't buy too much of any one investment option; don't have too much in the stock market. Spread your money across the savings and investment board.

"Don't play with sharp objects. You can hurt yourself." In the world of finance, people who make a commission on things they "recommend" are sharp objects. Don't play with them. Learn how to do it yourself or get help from a fee-only adviser who is a fiduciary (someone who must put the client first).

"Finish your homework." Mom wants you to do well in school. The financial reason is, a good education brings a good job and a good job brings benefits. Your financial life will be much better if you have a steady job, a good health care program, and good retirement benefits. Pick a career you enjoy. Enthusiasm is the key to success!

"Walk. Don't run." If you are going into something new in finances, walk; don't run. Take your time. Learn about it. Think about it. Do not make a hasty decision because some financial salesman bought you lunch. Apply the twenty-four-hour rule: when pressed to buy, tell the seller you need twenty-four hours to think it over.

"Eat your vegetables." Mom knows health is more important than wealth. Live a healthy life. Eat good stuff, exercise, and have many close relationships.

Thanks, Mom, for all your wisdom. Now, if we could only follow your advice.

A footnote about Dad: Kaitlyn, twenty-one, says, "I can relate to the advice of listening to your mom because my mother would always tell me to save when I was younger, and I did. Unfortunately, I listened to her so much that I would never spend any money. My dad had to sit me down and tell me that it was okay to spend sometimes, though I should never spend excessive amounts. I think that's an important lesson."

Live within Your Means: What Does That Mean?

I tell everybody, "Live within your means!" I'm often asked to further explain just what that entails. At the very basic level, this entails the following:

- **Live** = this refers to all the money you spend in a given period—for example, each month.
- **Within** = in this case, it means "less than."
- **Your means** = this refers to all your income, your take-home pay plus any other source that provides spending money.
- **Live within your means** = spend less than you make.

In the real world, in addition to your monthly expenses, it means you need to earn the following:

- Money to pay off your debts through regular monthly payments.
- Money for an emergency fund and money to refill that fund after it is used.
- Money saved for the future purchase of large items—house, car, things like that.
- Money set aside for retirement, your most important investment goal.

Indications that you are not living within your means include never having money left at the end of the month and/or not being able to pay off all credit card debt each month.

Your first step is to track your expenses by category and then compare total expenses to total income. This is a difficult step for many people, but it absolutely, positively is something you must figure out how to do.

If your budget is not balanced, the next steps by far are the most difficult. You must acknowledge you have a problem and change the way you handle your finances. Acknowledging the problem and making the effort to change seem to be the most difficult things people must accomplish. The hardest thing to get someone to say is

"I can't afford that." Practice out loud saying this. Then put together a list of things you cannot afford: a cable TV, fast food, gas at nine dollars a gallon. (I once figured that if you buy a gallon of gas on a credit card for three dollars and then make minimum payments, you end up paying nine dollars for each gallon of gas. And you are still paying for the gas long after it is used up.)

My advice is if you are not living within your means, look in a mirror and admit to yourself that it is not real smart to pay nine dollars a gallon for gas. Then accept full financial responsibility for yourself and your family, and begin to take the steps necessary to change the way you spend your money. It will be one of the best things you ever do!

Financial Goals: The How-To

Putting together financial goals is a very important part of personal finance. Many people say, "Financial goals? That sounds too difficult. I don't know where to begin." And then they do nothing. Here's how to come up with your financial goals:

Goals must be

1. written down,
2. achievable,
3. have a timeline,
4. precise.

The key to getting started is to begin small with easy goals. Once you accomplish simple goals, you can come up with more difficult goals.

If your goal is to start saving for retirement, write it down and list the timeline as "now." Then open your wallet and put a dollar bill into a (hopefully empty) coffee can. There you go. You have accomplished your goal to start saving for retirement. Flush with success, perhaps you can say, "I'm twenty-two, and I will put twenty-two dollars in my retirement can each week until I am twenty-three, and then I will put twenty-three dollars in each week."

Cutting back on spending can be a challenge, but the key again is to start with easy-to-accomplish goals. List your goal as "Before my next trip to the grocery story, I will write a list of things to buy, and I will stick to my list." Or have a goal to leave the kids home when you shop so they won't always be asking for things. Or tell the kids each can add one fruit to the grocery shopping list, nothing else. Simple and achievable.

Family finances should involve self-assessment. Put your cell phone down for fifteen to twenty minutes and think about your money life. Write down what you want to change. If you can't come up with any "shortcomings," ask someone who could tell you your shortcomings—that would be your spouse or partner. But make it a mutual exchange of one shortcoming each. Then drop the idea of being defensive, take a look at your shortcomings, think about ways to improve yourself, and write them down as goals.

Don't have goals that are too general, such as "I want a comfortable retirement." That's a wish, a desired outcome, not a goal. Start with "I will contribute to my company 401(k) so I'll receive the maximum matching contribution from my company." Then ask HR what contribution amount will receive the maximum match. (Remember to continue your cash contributions in the coffee can). Next, figure out your new take-home pay, and adjust your spending budget accordingly.

Once you succeed in reaching a goal, get into the habit of regularly thinking about your money and writing down additional goals. Your financial life will be much better if you plan ahead and have written financial goals.

The most important step in writing financial goals is to start!

When You Might Need a Money Coach

The following are scenarios when you might need a Money Coach:

- ☐ Your spouse thinks he/she should take the checkbook to the money market.
- ☐ You think retirement planning means looking at travel brochures.
- ☐ Like most people, you spend approximately ninety thousand hours working and ten hours planning your retirement.
- ☐ You don't have an up-to-date will.
- ☐ When it comes to money issues with your partner, one or both of you yell (and the kids hear it).
- ☐ Your monthly financial statements are stacked up unopened in a pile somewhere on your desk or ignored on your computer.
- ☐ You think IRA is one of the Marines who put up the flag on Iwo Jima.
- ☐ You bought your last mutual fund from a guy in a $1,200 suit.
- ☐ The guy in the $1,200 suit made more money than you did on the deal.
- ☐ Your teenager has a cell phone, and you pay the bill.
- ☐ Your savings plan consists of "putting aside" whatever is left at the end of the month.
- ☐ You can't pay off your credit cards.
- ☐ Your insurance agent doesn't call you for an annual meeting to review insurance coverage.
- ☐ You are a renter and don't have renters' insurance.
- ☐ You have one spouse, several children, one house, two cars, a retirement plan, and you don't have umbrella insurance.
- ☐ You think the number 529 means the area code where your child wants to attend college.
- ☐ Someone else prepares your taxes and doesn't explain line by line what the numbers mean.
- ☐ You don't know your credit score.
- ☐ You think financial planning only means investments.
- ☐ You think investing is too difficult for you to understand.

- ☐ You are not sure whether you are paying mortgage insurance.
- ☐ You think a tattoo is a need.
- ☐ You have no idea what "fiduciary" means.

Note: a Money Coach is someone who helps you with your money, someone who does not make a commission on an investment recommendation, someone on your side of the table, a fiduciary who puts you, the client, first.

Take the Money Coach Test: The Financial Checkup

As a Money Coach, I am a registered investment adviser (RIA) with the state of Colorado. That is my credential. But what I do is coach people and families about money matters. I educate. I advise. I encourage people to do the right things with their money. I congratulate success and give homework when there are shortfalls. Just like a track coach, I do not run the race. The person I coach runs the race. The person I coach does the work. It is up to you!

The first step with each new client is to ask a series of short questions. I call it the financial checkup. You and your family also will benefit from going through this financial checkup. After ten minutes, I can understand a person's financial situation and can then begin coaching them on financial matters. After ten minutes, you can understand your own financial situation better, and then move to make corrections. Take the test with your partner or spouse.

Let's start with the first and most important question.

Do you make more than you spend?

I am interested in the answer, the time it takes to answer, and the body language exhibited when giving the answer. With couples, I observe the interaction; it says a lot.

Other questions are the following:

- Is there anyone besides yourself whose future hinges on your financial decisions?
- What is the best financial decision you have made in your life?
- What is the worst financial decision you have made in your life?
- Do you pay off your credit card bill each month?
- Have you reviewed your credit reports in the past year?
- Do you have a written spending plan, something called a budget?
- Do you save part of your income each month?
- What have been your sources for learning about investing?
- What lessons have you learned about investing?

- ☐ What percentage are you contributing to your company retirement plan? What is the maximum company match? How much do you have in regular IRA and Roth IRA accounts?
- ☐ Do you know the asset allocation of your investments? Percentage in stocks, bonds, cash, property?
- ☐ Do you know the annual expense percentage of each investment?
- ☐ Do you own your home, or do you rent? What is the monthly payment?
- ☐ Has an expert reviewed your insurance coverage?
- ☐ Who does your taxes, and is there tax planning?

Answer these questions, and then act as your own Money Coach to put your financial world in better order. The key is common sense!

The Big Money Picture

Because I am a Money Coach, people often ask me questions about money matters. I tell one and all I need to know the big picture—the big money picture—before I address specific money issues.

I have had questions like the following:

- ☐ "How can the investments in my nephew's 401(k) be rebalanced?" But I don't know anything else about the nephew's financial situation. What regular investments does he have, and what are those investments?

- ☐ "I want to talk about investments but only after I buy a house." Can you afford the house?

- ☐ "Is putting more money in my 401(k) a good idea?" What is your level of debt?

- ☐ "My financial adviser manages my money." Does your financial adviser know your big money picture? Is he really working for you?

The message: When you make decisions on your personal finances, you must first consider your own big money picture. How will this choice affect other parts of your money world? Do you have enough background information on this matter to make a good decision?

Most of us don't spend enough time managing our money world. Many have little idea what their big money picture is. Put big money picture on your to-do list, and figure it out. Eventually, you will reach the conclusion that you are the one who best knows your big picture. Then take charge of your personal finances; don't let anyone else do it for you.

A Money Exercise for All

Write down three things you believe you have done right with your money. Then write down three things you want to know about money matters. Study the list. Congratulate yourself on the positive. Seek nonbiased answers on the things you want to know. Next year, do it again.

List here three things you have done right with your money:
1.

2.

3.

List here three things you really want to know about money:
1.

2.

3.

Learn from Kids

I talk to kids about money all the time. It is interesting to compare their comments on money to the money problems faced by many Americans.

Third-grader Diego, eight, puts 40% of any money he receives in his "Save for College" jar. Small start, but a big first step in the right direction. He puts the remaining 60% into a piggy bank for future purchases. Diego told me he makes a big mistake if he spends all his available money on spur-of-the-moment wants, like candy. He sets aside a very small amount of cash for his sweet tooth. His focus is on things he really needs. He spends a lot of time thinking about these bigger items and puts them in a list and changes the list to meet his current priority. He asks his mom to tell him no if he asks for candy while shopping. He then asks to look at the things on his priority list.

Years ago, I asked Melissa (ten, fourth grade) and her brother Michael (eight, second grade), "What is money?" Like the majority of adults, they got it half right: "Money is a piece of paper that you buy stuff with." Money is actually a medium of exchange; it is earned, and then it can be spent. In the old days, a cowboy worked on a ranch in exchange for food and a place to stay. The modern cowboy exchanges work for money and then exchanges the money for food and a place to stay. Both kids did understand the concept of earning money by doing work.

Each told me they receive an allowance. I asked them what they had to do in exchange for the allowance. They answered, "I make my bed, clean my room, and put my clothes away." I asked what they did with their money. They said, "I put it in my ATM."

I said, "You mean your piggy bank?"

"No, my ATM."

I went upstairs and saw that each had a mini ATM. It had an access card and a PIN; money goes in, and the ATM gives them the balance of their savings. Mom said when they wanted something, she'd ask, "How much do you have in your ATM?"

The concept of earning money and saving money is very important for young children, as is the concept that the amount in your ATM is limited to what you put in.

"What if you had two dollars and wanted to buy something for four dollars?" I asked.

Melissa answered, "I would save."

Michael said, "I would ask my mom for two dollars more."

Mom, of course, would ask about the money in the ATM. Their responses show they understood they could not buy something unless they had the money.

"What would you tell your classmates about money?" I asked.

Melissa answered, "Use it wisely."

Michael said, "Save it."

At the conclusion of my Junior Achievement class for sixth graders, I asked them to give me some advice for my TV audience. They came up with these gems:

☐ Never spend more than what you have.
☐ When you go shopping, don't spend more than what you have in your pocket.
☐ Don't spend as much as you have; save some.
☐ Set money aside for emergencies.

Hats off to these youngsters. Here's the good news for you: it is never too late to learn the basics about money.

CHAPTER 2

Money by the Numbers

Ten Facts about Your Money Life

Two Must-Know Things about Your Money

Eight Rules for Financial Success

Ten Things Young Professionals Need to Know about Money

Six Steps to Financial Survival after a Job Loss

Ten Facts about Your Money Life

Fact 1: Financial planning is **taking responsibility** for your own money. You cannot delegate this responsibility to your spouse or a financial person. Yes, work with your spouse. Yes, work with a Money Coach. But ultimately, you—and only you—are responsible for your money life.

Fact 2: Money management is **mainly common sense**. It does not depend on your level of education; it depends on your smarts. If I were to borrow your pen, you would expect me to return it. If you borrow money from a credit card or a bank, the credit card or the bank would expect you to return the money.

Fact 3: Having the right **attitude** is necessary for success in anything, especially money management. The single most powerful asset we have is our mind. Financial aptitude is knowing what you do with the money once you make it, how to keep people from taking it from you, how long you keep it, and how hard that money works for you.

Fact 4: **Save a little on a regular basis** for a long time. "Savings" should be your first category in your budget. Put money into savings first.

Fact 5: It's not how much you make; **it's how much you spend**. You don't have full control of how much you make; you do control how much you spend. Start by keeping track of every dollar you spend. Then put together a budget based on your income and your goals. Follow that budget when buying things.

Fact 6: Beginning with modest assets and **building a fortune obviously requires thrift**. When you find yourself in a hole, stop digging. How do you spot a millionaire? He/she turns off the light when leaving the room.

Fact 7: Understand the **value of compounding**. An eighty-year-old moved out of her home; $80,000 in pennies were found—a lot of money, about $100 a month. If that $100 were put into a bank savings account at 4% interest compounded annually, the total would have been $185,000. If the $100 had been invested, the total would have been in the millions. Make your money work for you.

Fact 8: **Protect your credit**. Pay your bills on time. Avoid credit cards. Buy something only if you have the money in the bank.

Fact 9: **Retirement** is your most important investment goal. For every day you work now, the money earned must pay for that day and for some day in the future when you will not have earned income. Social Security (if it survives) will take care of perhaps 40% of your budget. You must save for the rest.

Fact 10: You cannot do financial planning without **understanding your taxes** and the tax system. Taxes most likely will be higher in the future. Pay taxes now, not later. For retirement, open a Roth account. Contributions and earnings are not taxed when withdrawn in retirement.

It's your money. Learn how to manage it!

Two Must-Know Things about Your Money

Here are two must-know things about managing your money.

First, what is a **fiduciary**, and why do you need one? "Fiduciary" means "trust," and it means the financial person must put you, the client, first. As a registered investment adviser and Money Coach, I am a fiduciary. I do not sell financial products. Many financial people hem and haw when asked, "Are you a fiduciary?" I work for the best interest of the client; I do not make recommendations based on any personal benefit. If you are just starting or have been investing for half a century, ask your financial person to notify you in writing of any instance in which he/she will not be acting as a fiduciary.

Second, be aware of your **credit score**. I belong to a Facebook group called Word of Mouth, Colorado Springs. It has twenty-five thousand citizens posting all sorts of questions and comments. I am concerned because I see many questions starting with "I have bad credit, and I need to buy something." As a Money Coach, I say the answer is simple. Fix your bad credit now:

☐ **Identify your problem**. It is most often overspending and/or lack of an adequate emergency fund. Stop spending! Build your emergency fund!

☐ Once you figure out your own problem, **resolve to fix it**.

☐ **Declare a financial emergency**, and put all your effort into fixing your credit.

The main component of your credit score is paying your bills on time. If you can't pay off your credit card at the end of the month, stop using your credit card. If your income is less than your spending level, you have two choices:

1. Spend less money.
2. Make more money.

Borrowing is **not** an option.

If you are in real financial trouble—no place to stay, nothing to eat—call 211 (this is for Colorado Springs, so check your area) and ask for help.

Most people who make these posts have made poor money decisions. And I fear if they don't get that wake-up call, they are going to continue to make poor money decisions, like

- ☐ not tracking expenses/having no idea where their money goes,
- ☐ receiving food stamps yet spending hundreds of dollars a month on fast food,
- ☐ paying to have the car washed,
- ☐ cable TV, and
- ☐ spending on wants, not needs.

I want this to be a wake-up call for all those who do not have good credit. Don't find a way around it. Fix it!

Eight Rules for Financial Success

Rule 1: Have **financial goals**. The goals must be precise, achievable, and have a timeline. And they must be written. We spend more time planning our next two-week vacation than we spend planning thirty years of retirement—this is not right.

Rule 2: If you have a spouse or partner, you must hold regularly scheduled **money talks** to discuss how your family finances work and how to improve your money life.

Rule 3: You must **make more money than you spend**. The way to make sure you do this is to categorize and track your expenses and compare the total expenses to your total net income. Do every month. Track every dollar spent.

Rule 4: **Manage your debt** carefully. If you use a credit card, you must pay it off at each billing cycle. Your house is not a source of cash to close the gap because of overspending. Pay down your mortgage so you will not have a house payment when you retire.

Rule 5: You must have an **emergency fund**, a safe pile of cash from which to pay your bills if your income falters. Start with six months of bare-bones expenses (only needs, not wants).

Rule 6: **Pay yourself first**. Save/invest a percentage of money each month before you pay the bills—at least 10% of your total income. The more, the better.

Rule 7: **Do not use a "windfall" of cash** (tax refund, IRA withdrawal, inheritance, lottery win) **to pay off a money problem** (overspending, for example) without first solving the money problem (stop overspending).

Rule 8: **Manage your investments carefully**. Have savings and investments both in retirement accounts and in regular accounts. Diversify your investments (called asset allocation—some in stocks, some in bonds, some in cash, some in "other.") Determine a percentage to be held in each category and then rebalance your holdings annually.

Ten Things Young Professionals Need to Know about Money

Fact 1: **Okay, now you are an adult**. When it comes to your money, you have choices. You can do things that will benefit you now and in the years ahead or you can do things that will harm you. Your task is to know the difference and make the right decisions. It's your money! Think before you act! Use common sense! Be responsible!

Fact 2: **Work with others**; learn from others. If you have a spouse, schedule regular money meetings. Friends can be savings buddies or investing buddies. Find a mentor. Avoid those trying to sell you stuff. Put down that cell phone and talk to people face-to-face about money.

Fact 3: List five things you have done right with your money so far. List five areas for improvement. What five things would you tell your peers about money? Reflect on what you have written. Discuss with friends. **Write a plan** outlining changes you will make to improve. Follow the plan.

Fact 4: Take note of **credit and debt**. Never spend more money than you make. If you are short, you have two choices: make more or spend less. Borrow only to buy things that go up in value (house, education), not things that go down in value (car, groceries, clothes, etc.). Do not use a credit card if you cannot pay off the balance at the end of the month.

Fact 5: **The best investment is education**. But don't waste your time in college. Get the most of your educational involvement. Study, study, study, and think, think, think. Work hard at learning as much as you can. However, make sure your education equals work because the secret to making money is going to work, and make sure you can pay off all student debt in two to three years.

Fact 6: **Protect your assets**. Know the types of insurance you need and the types you don't.

Fact 7: **Track your expenses** each month or pay period. You must know where your money goes. Then decide if your spending is in line with your income and your goals.

Fact 8: **Save! Save! Save!** Put aside money from each paycheck for the future.

Fact 9: **Kids watch everything you do**. When it comes to family finances and you have children, set the example. Do it right; then the kids will learn to do it right.

Fact 10: **Invest**. The financial industry wants to "manage" your money because it is "too complicated" for you. Wrong! Learn the basics of investing, and do it yourself.

Six Steps to Financial Survival after a Job Loss

Step 1: **Don't panic**. Job loss is a fact of life; just about everyone loses a job at some point in his or her work life. You will survive, and things may even turn out for the better. Keep your family informed of what is happening. Let them know family income has been affected and family expenditures will be affected. Seek cooperation from family and friends. Show strength and leadership to your family; let them know things will be okay.

Step 2: Understand what your former employer is offering. The idea is to maximize your income from this employer. Offer to work part time beyond the termination date; explore the possibility of consulting work; ask what you need to do to extend health benefits. Add severance pay to your emergency fund and start your emergency budget at once. Make sure you get a letter of recommendation from your former employer. Don't burn any bridges; be remembered as a good, responsible worker. Think smart. As a hiring manager I will not give points to an applicant who has a silly voice mail message or to a phone conversation with marginal reception quality. Call your own cell phone and listen to what your hiring manager hears.

Step 3: Apply for unemployment and look for a new job right away. Understand it probably will take you longer than anticipated to find a new source of income. Calculate how much unemployment you will receive and determine when the first check will arrive. Factor the unemployment amount into your emergency family budget and make the necessary adjustments so that you do not spend more than you have. Be creative in your job search; network widely; put volunteer time into your schedule; reassess your career and obtain new skills and education now that you have the time.

Step 4: Make intelligent decisions about retirement accounts and insurance. Keep your health insurance through COBRA. Don't drop life insurance; you want to prevent an even larger family financial disaster. Keep paying for home and auto policies. These expenditures are part of your bare bones budget. Don't touch your retirement savings.

Step 5: Develop an emergency spending plan, your budget while unemployed. First, review all sources of possible income: part-time work, garage sale (we all have stuff we no longer need or simply can't afford to keep), rent from a roommate, loans from family and friends, money from returning the new wide-screen TV, and others (list your creative ideas here). Next, review all spending. Less is better when income is down. Many families continue to spend as if nothing has changed. Think downsize, especially where you live and what you drive. Your family now can buy only the essentials—no new clothing, no eating out. Cancel your cable TV. Stop using credit cards (cash only). The kids can drink tap water. Move away from processed foods at the grocery store. Eat cheap; eat healthy. The hard part is changing spending habits. Just about everyone can use an "extreme makeover" when it comes to where we spend our money and how we pay for things. Your time is now.

Step 6: Keep your chin up, and exercise a lot; things will be better.

CHAPTER 3

Buying Stuff

How to Track Family Expenses and Put Together a Budget

I Have an Emergency Fund—Do You?

Food and Your Budget

Control Your Spending

Buying Your First Home?

How to Buy a Car

Should I Buy a Timeshare?

It's not
how much
you make.
It's how much
you spend!

Money
save, save, save,
not
spend,
spend,
spend!

How to Track Family Expenses and Put Together a Budget

The **most important** action you can take with your personal or your family's finances is to accurately track expenditures. When you know exactly where your money goes, you can redirect your spending patterns to fit your goals. This is the road to financial success.

The first step is to list your spending categories. Spending categories very much depend on your situation. Categories must be broad enough to help you view various segments of your spending. But there should not be too many categories, or you will create a bureaucratic challenge.

Here are some suggested categories (subcategories): shelter (mortgage/rent, maintenance and upkeep, utilities, phone, internet); food (groceries, eating out, fast food, coffee); clothes (his, hers, the kids'); transportation (car payment, gas, licensing, insurance, maintenance); personal care (his, hers, the kids'); medical (co-pay, RX, dental); gifts and donations; and miscellaneous. Walmart, for example, is not a category because you can buy items that fit into a wide variety of categories. Interest payments are not a category because you should be paying your credit card off at the end of each month. Write down your categories on a page or two of paper with plenty of room between items, or accomplish the same setup using your computer, iPad, or iPhone.

The next step is for each family member to keep a record of all the money spent each day. This can be accomplished on a blank notepad, the use of receipts or check stubs, or with the help of various apps such as Budget Envelopes, Budgeting Tool, or Budgets. Periodically (daily, weekly, twice a month) transfer the list of expenditures to the proper place on your categories sheet. Total each category at the end of the month, then total all categories, and subtract the sum from your total net income. The figure should be a positive number. In other words, you should have spent less than you've made.

Once a month, you or all family members should review the expenses and ask yourselves, "Is this where our money should go?"

Also understand that you can exercise control over all expenses—yes, even the house or car payment (you can always downsize, upsize, or refinance), and yes, the other needs as well, like utilities (turn off the lights) or clothes (you "need" clothes for work and play, but you don't need thirty-two pairs of shoes). Don't look at wants as a bad thing. Once you have a balanced budget and have cash set aside for an emergency fund, for retirement, and for other long-term goals, you or your family can spend as much as it can afford on things listed as wants.

Tracking expenses and putting together a budget are closely related.

Tracking expenses is a look backward at how much money you have spent in each spending category. Once you know your level of spending, you can determine if the money spent fits your income and your lifestyle and your goals.

Putting together a budget is a look forward. A budget is based on your average spending in each category (from tracking expenses) and your available income. In your budget, you project future spending amounts for each category based on past spending and future estimated spending.

For those whose income is close to expenditures (or income is lower than expenditures), a budget provides guidelines on the maximum amount you can spend in each budget category. You must stop spending when you reach your budgeted spending limit, or you must take money out of other categories to address the shortfall. For those whose income is more (or much more) than expenditures, a budget provides a comprehensive view of spending so you can better address your overall financial goals. If you are a compulsive saver and you are reluctant to spend money, your budget can provide an incentive to spend a bit more in categories where your limits are higher than your actual expenditures.

And for unexpected and unanticipated expenses, you must have available cash outside the budget for expenses not in the budget. This is your emergency fund.

Tracking expenses and putting together a budget—just do these.

I Have an Emergency Fund—Do You?

As a financial adviser and Money Coach, I am always hammering home the idea that each person/each family must have an emergency fund to deal with expenses that are not in the monthly budget. A client once asked me about my emergency fund. He wanted to know if I practice what I preach.

I do follow my own guidance. I have an emergency fund and replenish it immediately when it is used. In fact, I have three emergency funds—one for unplanned expenses; two for medical emergencies.

Emergency fund number 1 is for unexpected expenses that are not in the budget. This is for things like car repair, replacing a broken TV, traveling to visit a sick relative. How much should someone have in his/her emergency fund? That depends on your specific circumstances. The three-to-six-month standard does not apply to all people. Since my income is reasonably solid and does not depend on working for someone else, I don't need to cover a set number of months of bare-bone expenses should I lose my job. The money in this emergency fund resides in an online bank account that currently provides interest at the rate of 2.2% (as of February 2019)—not great, but better than my checking account, where money sits at 0%.

Emergency fund number 2 is for medical emergencies. I have health insurance, but I don't have dental insurance. This fund covers any large deductibles or co-pays I may encounter as well as dental emergencies over and above regular cleanings. Have I ever used this medical emergency fund? Ask the guy who gave me a root canal last year. This money also is in my online bank account. It can be quickly transferred to my checking account.

Emergency fund number 3 holds money I hope I will never need for long-term care expenses. The goal for this fund is two years' worth of nursing home care at $60,000 per year. The money is in I-Bonds, a US government savings bond, which is inflation protected. (One caution on the use of I-Bonds is that they cannot be redeemed for one year after purchase.) I'm building up my I-Bond account each year. The maximum purchase of I-Bonds per year is $10,000. November 2018 interest rate is 2.83%; May 2019 interest rate is 1.90%.

How many emergency funds do you have?

Food and Your Budget

Food is a need, a necessity, a must-have. When reviewing your food expenses, you might think you don't need to change how you eat or cut this portion of the budget. Wrong! Americans waste about a pound of food a day (according to a USDA study) or about 20% of all food purchases. Wasting food is wasting money. Below are some food tips from Liz, a nutritionist in training and one who manages the family budget closely.

The following are money-saving tips on buying food:
- Do buy in bulk
- Do buy on sale
- Do sign up for store rewards and discount cards
- Do plan your meals in advance
- Do make a shopping list before you go to the store
- Do not shop hungry
- Do not take the kids unless you make a deal with them on saving money. Share the savings with your kids
- Do use the smaller cart
- Do not buy on impulse
- Do visit multiple stores to get the best deals
- Do cook at home; eat out less
- Do plant a garden
- Do freeze food to preserve it

The following are tips on the kinds of food to eat:
- Do cook mostly from scratch
- Do buy plenty of fresh or frozen fruits and vegetables
- Do buy plenty of healthy fats (avocado, olive oil, coconut butter, nut butter)
- Do not buy too many prepackaged, highly processed foods
- Do read the labels. Steer clear of added sugars, oils, soy, and ingredients that you cannot identify or pronounce
- Do buy full-fat dairy (butter, milk, yogurt, cheese)
- Do not center your diet around processed grains, like cereals and breads

☐ Do not default to low-fat, high-sugar/high-carb snacks (which are designed to keep you hungry so you will buy more)

☐ Do invest in herbs and seasonings to give your food a variety of flavors

Remember the following:

☐ Food costs money. Don't waste food; don't waste money

☐ Being healthy is more important than being wealthy

Control Your Spending

Shopping

- ☐ Know what you want to buy ahead of time. Make a list. No impulse purchases.
- ☐ Shop when you feel good. Wear comfortable clothing. Shop early in the day.
- ☐ Don't shop with someone who doesn't like to shop. Leave someone like me at home.
- ☐ Do not apply for store credit cards.
- ☐ Don't wait until the last minute. Avoid priority shipping costs.
- ☐ Apply for rebates. Get a gift receipt. Do not get extended warrantees.

Buying Gifts

Start with a budget. Before you start shopping, sit down and figure out what your gift budget will be. If you want a starting point, I suggest gifts be about 1% of the family income: $30,000 a year equals $300; $65,000 equals $650.

Pay for gifts with cash. Take out the amount of your gift budget in cash. The first advantage is that you will not overspend; second is that you will have already paid for the gifts. There will be no credit card bill in January.

If you haven't saved up the cash this year, then make it a point to put aside money from each paycheck for next Christmas.

Look for appropriate and inexpensive gifts. Think of the person receiving the gift, and determine something he or she would really like. Don't buy things you like; buy things they will appreciate. Keep a record of gifts given in years past so you won't repeat gifts.

Gifts need not be expensive. The best gifts are things you make yourself. My sister likes to work with her hands. She will buy a reasonably priced jacket and then personalize it with a name. If you take good photos, present one as a gift. Bake things.

What would a Money Coach want from his kids? I would be overjoyed to get a note that says: "Dear Dad, this year in your honor, I put an extra [amount in dollars] in my Roth IRA. Merry Christmas." I would just love that!

Shut Down Your Spending

In the aftermath of the government shutdown in January 2018, several people told me they too were shutting down personal spending. Martha has advised me that she is stopping or deferring purchases to reduce expenses. She will save the money and put it aside for upcoming travel (called saving for a purpose).

Here are some of her ideas:

☐ Not going to any store to spend any money, even online, until the next payday

☐ Planning meals with food already in the house and writing down possible menus (less wasted food with this plan)

☐ Wearing more clothes when it's cold (to reduce the heating bill), saving the initial colder water when taking a bath to water plants, flushing less often (to reduce the water bill), turning off the lights not in use (to reduce the electricity bill), combining errands (to save gasoline)

☐ Never buying things from the end of the aisle, a place where stores want to catch your eye and make you buy something not on your written shopping list

My Recommendations as a Money Coach

Your nonemotional self must be in control when it comes to buying stuff. Be a lender, not a borrower. Shop less often. Think before you buy anything. Ask yourself, "Is there a better future use for these dollars?"

We all should be more frugal when managing our family's finances. But please do not try to model yourself after the federal government when it comes to managing your money!

Buying Your First Home?

Here's What You Need to Know

Goal: you want to buy a house—someday. The key word is "someday." You must plan ahead, years and years ahead, if your goal is to buy a house. You planned and saved for college; it is the same process for buying a house. You've planned and prepared and interviewed for your first job; it is the same process for buying a house. You cannot just decide "I will buy a house" despite having a low-to-mid credit score, limited savings, and little knowledge of the process.

It is essential to have your personal finances under control:

☐ More money coming in than going out.
☐ You must know where your money goes. You need a budget. And your budget must include savings and investing.
☐ Your debt should be minimal. Know how to use a credit card. If you carry credit card debt month to month, solve that problem before thinking about buying a house.
☐ You must have a substantial emergency fund.
☐ You need money in the bank and a savings plan.
☐ And your credit score must be good.

Bottom line: you must be able to afford a home before you start the process.

If you loan money to a friend, your concern is whether the friend will pay you back. (Note: this is an example; do **not** loan money to friends.) If the bank loans money to you, the bank wants assurance you will pay the money back. The bank checks your credit score. The credit score is much more than a number. Your score affects your interest rate, your insurance rate, your ability to get a job, etc. You **must** have a good, very good, or excellent score before you buy.

There are two cost categories when buying a house:

1. Initial one-time costs: moving, getting rid of old stuff, buying new things, changing addresses, down payment,

inspections, various fees connected with the mortgage, closing costs, registration fees. At purchase, you should put down as much as possible, avoid mortgage insurance, and limit closing costs. Don't skimp on the home inspection.

2. Monthly or periodic recurring fees: mortgage and mortgage insurance, property taxes, home insurance, utilities, maintenance, homeowners association fee.

When You Are Financially Ready

The following advice is from former client Kristina, a successful real estate agent who bought her first home at twenty-six and now owns four investment properties yielding monthly income.

Once you are financially ready, ask yourself these questions:

1. "What is my current living situation?" Can you easily break your lease with little penalty?

2. "Will I need to move too soon to justify purchasing a home?" It doesn't make sense to buy a house if you know you will have to move in the near future, unless you plan to be an investor and rent out the house. If you plan to keep this first house, how will you pay for the next house?

3. "Am I mentally ready to buy a house?" When you start thinking about buying a house, it's easy to follow your heart instead of your head and get caught up in the awe of looking at houses. Don't fall prey to this! The worst thing you can do is contact a real estate agent and start looking at houses you may or may not be able to afford, which not only is a waste of everyone's time but can be a huge disappointment if you find something you really like but cannot afford.

4. "What are the benefits of home ownership over renting, including the 'penalty' of any type of mortgage insurance?" In most cases, the long-term benefit and savings are worth the cost of the insurance.

How to Start

Here are the steps on how to start:

1. First, speak to a mortgage lender or your bank to see what kind of loan you qualify for and what kind of payment amounts would suit your comfort level. Call the lender and state you are looking to be prequalified (down the road, you'll be preapproved, which is a much more formal process) for a home mortgage, and provide them the minimum details required to determine your buying power. You are not locked in with them at this time, but this is an essential step.

2. Do your homework. There are many programs for first-time home buyers that may not require the conventional 20% down necessary to avoid mortgage insurance. Bear in mind that the mortgage company will not tell you right away when you have satisfied the mortgage insurance requirement after a number of years. It is up to you to request termination of mortgage insurance when you are eligible. Depending on your profession, look into VA loans and specialty programs for teachers, firefighters, law enforcement, and doctors.

Moving Forward Once You Are Prequalified

Once you are prequalified, you can do the following:

1. Find the right real estate agent. Talk to friends and family and get a referral to an agent who works full-time in the business, is familiar with the area you are looking into, and will listen to your needs and communicate with you such that you feel you are their only client. Remember, the agent is being paid by the seller in most cases, so this is one cost that does not come out of your pocket. Interview three to five agents, and check out each online.

2. Work with your agent to understand the requirements for your new home—whether you need a fence, how big the

MONEY SENSE FOR YOUNG PROFESSIONALS

garage is, if it's close to work, if proximity to schools is important, how many bedrooms there are, etc.

3. Select an agent, and start looking at houses that meet your criteria. Know your deal breakers.

The Home-Buying Process

The following are the processes involved in buying a home:

1. Once you find the right house, your agent will help you define and submit an offer. The dates are imperative, especially if you are breaking a lease or need to work around specific dates. The price you can pay is important. Make sure to think this through when outlining the offer with your agent. If negotiations get intense, remember you want to buy this home and they want to sell it. Prepare to overlook decor and paint colors. Those can be changed with minimal cost, but the right location, price, and other requirements cannot be overlooked. Your agent will help with this.

2. When under contract, your agent will help you determine what inspections you should consider and/or if a survey is necessary. At minimum, perform a general home inspection. Remember, it is the home inspector's job to find things wrong with the house, so don't overreact when you receive a long report of issues. Working with your agent, you can determine if it's best to walk away or to negotiate some sort of resolution and move forward. Other inspections, like those for termite or radon, may be relevant; your agent will guide you. When the time is right, you will want the lender to order the appraisal so you can move toward final loan approval. The appraisal is ordered by the bank and protects you from paying more than the home's true value. If the appraisal comes in lower than your offer price, your real estate agent can provide the best guidance for what to do next. The lender will also ask you to obtain homeowner's insurance for the property at this time.

3. The words you are waiting to hear from the lender at this point are "clear to close." You will receive a copy of your closing documents to review in advance of closing day. Review them with your agent, as sometimes there are errors and/or adjustments that need to be made. The costs of interest are the closing costs, prorated property taxes, HOA fee (if applicable), and your homeowner's insurance. These documents will also tell you how much money you need to have transferred before the day of closing.

4. Next, perform a final walkthrough with your agent to make sure the house is in good condition and has been left as agreed. Then close on your home. Additionally, your agent will remind you when the time is right to have utilities transferred to your name.

5. Grab the keys, move in, and start enjoying home ownership.

How to Buy a Car

As we all know, the secret to making money is going to work. In this article, the operative word is "go." You must have reliable transportation in order to go to work. Public transportation, a trusted car pool, Uber or Lyft, or your own automobile are ways to get to work and back. If you need or want a car, here's advice on how to buy your transportation.

First question: **"Can I afford to buy a car?"**
You must know how much you make and how much you spend. You need to track all your current monthly expenses to the dollar and then compare that figure to your monthly net income and your goals. How much is available for transportation? Now, do the research on the cost of your car. Consider contemplated purchase price plus tax plus other purchase fees; monthly car payments, including interest (if you are not able to buy with cash); insurance (monthly or every six months); gas (how many miles will you drive, miles per gallon, price per gallon); annual registration and license fees; annual maintenance (oil change, estimate annual fixes). Make sure your car uses regular gas or is a hybrid or uses electric power only; avoid premium gas. Often the total cost of a car is twice the monthly car payments. Do the research before you start looking.

Determine if you can afford a new car or a used car. Remember, if your budget only permits a used car, you must buy a reliable used car. Do not jeopardize your job by failing to show up for work because your car keeps breaking down. If you cannot afford a car at this time, put money aside each paycheck for future purchase. Use another means to get to work until you have saved enough to buy your own car.

Remember, an automobile is a depreciating asset. It goes down in value over time, but your monthly payment stays the same. If at all possible, save the entire payment so you do not need to finance the car. It is best to only finance an appreciating asset like a house or an education.

Second question: **"What kind of car should I buy?"**

Buy a car that meets your needs and your budget. Do not buy an SUV or a pickup truck if you don't need an SUV or a pickup truck. Many people buy too much automobile. Don't make that mistake. A car should fit your specific transportation requirements; it should not be a status symbol. Figure out what you need, and then do the research on the type of car fits that need. Ask friends to let you drive around the block in their car. Every time you are outside, look at parked cars to determine make, color, and features. The goal is to select the exact car you want to own and can afford before you show up at the dealership.

Here are suggestions on making the buying process easier:

1. If you are going to finance the car, check with your bank/ credit union and insurance company before you contact a car dealer. Ask others who financed their automobiles. Note well that your credit score is considered on the interest rate of the loan and on your automobile insurance. Pay off debts and pay all your bills on time. Also, know that you can refinance a car loan. Search the web; compare refinancing rates at LendingTree.com.

2. Select the exact make, model, and year. Research the price for your car. Consumer Reports evaluates automobiles, both new and used, and the magazine has a service to assist car buyers (small fee). Check the internet for other sources on pricing.

3. Go to a dealership. Ask to test-drive "your car." Tell the salesperson you are looking at cars but that you do not intend to buy a car at this time. Ask that the dealership not do a credit check for this test drive (multiple credit checks while looking for a car can affect your credit score adversely). Check online sources for "your car."

4. Once you are comfortable and convinced that this is the car you want, call the salesperson at the dealership and request his/her best and final price. Then call/email all other dealerships within one hundred miles and request pricing. Most often, your local dealer will match or beat

the price of any other dealership. Again, check the internet for best pricing.

5. The worst part of buying a car in my experience is the "sign the papers" day. Check to see if your dealership has concierge service, where they deliver the car and sign the papers at your home. If you must go in and sign, tell the salesperson in advance that you will give the document person no more than twenty minutes. Otherwise the document person will spend several hours trying to sell you more stuff. Tell him/her that this is the price you have agreed upon and you will only consider price reductions. Then take control and turn the conversation to how you can drive out with additional savings.

The final thing to remember with your new (or used car) is pay full attention to driving your car safely. Do not use a cell phone or electronic device while driving even if it is hands-free. Your life and the lives of others depend on you being a safe and attentive driver.

A list of online resources for buying a car is available in the Resources section of this book.

Should I Buy a Timeshare?

I don't think a timeshare is a good way to spend your money. It has to do with the five "highs" and one "hard."

☐ High pressure
☐ High cost
☐ High interest rates
☐ High fees
☐ High improbability that you will want a vacation place like this in the years ahead
☐ Hard to sell

High pressure. High-pressure sales tactics are employed. It's like a used-car salesman on steroids.

High cost. Consider property value. You pay $15,000 for one week. Add fifty-one weeks—that's $780,000 a year. Is the place plus the pool plus activities really worth that much?

High interest rates. Mortgage interest on timeshares can be very high.

High fees. Maintenance fees and taxes typically run an additional $600–$800 a year. Fees rise 2.5 times inflation. Then there is a fee to join the exchange organization and another fee to make the exchange. This could add another $400. And in Hawaii, a friend had to pay an additional fee to turn on the air conditioner.

High improbability that you will want a vacation place like this in the years ahead. You are stuck with the concept of one week per year in the same place (unless you pay extra to change). This might be okay when the kids are toddlers. But will it work when they are teenagers or you are empty nesters?

Hard to sell. There are many more sellers than buyers. The question I most often hear is "How do I get rid of it?" In a divorce, it is "I want the dog. You can have the timeshare."

Is Timeshare an Investment?

A timeshare is definitely **not** an investment. If you try to sell your $15,000 timeshare, the offer might be $2,500, an 85% drop in value.

Here are alternatives to timeshares:

□ Renting someone else's timeshare for about the same as the annual fee

□ House exchange programs

□ Airbnb

Want to Sell Your Timeshare?

Never pay a fee upfront. First, see if the timeshare owner will buy the property back. There is a Timeshare Users Group that may provide useful information on the process. Do not just walk away from the timeshare. Finally, pass on the lesson learned to friends and relatives.

Be Careful Not to Inherit an Unwanted Timeshare

Don't have your parents put your name on the timeshare deed. If you receive an unwanted timeshare by the death of the owner, take note. If the timeshare is "right to use," the representative should inform the resort so the resort can take the timeshare back. If the timeshare has a real estate deed, file a disclaimer with the probate court.

Bottom Line

Timeshares are like boats. It is not a good idea to own one, but it is a good idea to have a friend who has one.

CHAPTER 4

Credit and Debt

When you are
in a hole,
stop digging!

Because
it is
your money!

How to Establish Credit

Credit is "the provision of money, goods, or services with the expectation of future payment." Key wording is "expectation of future payment." The person or entity you borrow from wants evidence you can and will pay them back.

How do you become eligible to borrow money if you are just starting out and have no history of paying borrowed funds back? You put your own money in a bank or credit union, and then you borrow the financial institution's money and pay it back with your money already on deposit.

Here's how: My credit union has a credit builder account whereby you deposit, for example, $1,000. Then you borrow $1,000 as a personal load from the credit union and use your deposited $1,000 to pay it back. Interest rates at the time of this writing ranged between 2.99% and 4%. So you actually should deposit a little more than you borrow so you can pay off the loaned money and the interest.

My bank has a secured credit card. You deposit a minimum of $300 in the bank and use that money or other money to pay off your monthly secured credit card charges. If you use the deposited $300 to pay off the monthly bill, you must put more money in the account to keep the balance at $300. If you use other money to pay off the monthly bill, your initial deposit remains $300 and covers future spending. There is an annual fee of $39 for the credit card, but most use this method only six to twelve months. Once you successfully pay off your secured credit card for the designated time period, you are eligible for a real credit card, which is not backed by your deposit.

During the "credit builder" or "secured credit card" period, the financial institution reports to the three credit bureaus that you are paying back the loan or paying your credit card balance. Thus, you are establishing credit.

Some credit cards companies like Deserve will open new accounts for those without a credit history. They use factors other than a credit score. Check out Deserve Classic.

If you have problems paying back this money loaned to you, you must understand you are not yet ready to "establish credit." Acknowledge your mistakes, correct them, and try again.

One result of establishing credit is a credit score. CreditKarma. com provides a free credit score. Your credit score is important for more than just using a credit card or buying a car or a house. Your credit history is checked by employers and insurance companies. Your goal is to have a very good to excellent credit score, generally 720 plus (note that there are several scales).

Debt and credit cards are the financial downfall of too many people. Know that credit is best used if paid off monthly without the addition of high interest charges (credit card) or money borrowed on an appreciating asset (such as your home). Do your research; check with your bank or credit union.

Once you establish credit, pay all your bills on time. Whether you pay your bills on time is 35% of your credit score. The next biggest aspect is debt levels, at 30%. If your credit card maximum is $1,000, keep your debt level at $100–$200. Do not max out your card and move to another.

Knowing how to use and manage credit and debt are extremely important to your financial life!

A Credit Card and You

Debt enables you to obtain items that you otherwise could not buy.

Debt creates an obligation to repay, limits cash outflows that otherwise would have been available for consumption or savings, and increases expenses through interest and finance charges.

Debt is best for large purchases. Every item, except a home and education, is a depreciating asset. A depreciating asset is an item that is used up and gone (food/gas) or the item (automobile) is worth less the longer you hold it. Try not to use credit to purchase a depreciating asset.

Credit cards should be used for convenience only and should be paid off monthly.

Recommendation: ACC. **Avoid Credit Cards**.

Credit cards are the downfall of many people.

When you don't pay off your credit card total monthly, you are making a huge mistake. Stop using the credit card and pay off the remaining debt as quickly as possible.

The mall wants you to have credit cards so you will spend, spend, spend. Think carefully about each purchase. Each time you buy something, ask yourself, "Can I afford this, and do I really need this?"

Alternatives are prepaid spending card, debit card, cash. Better yet—don't spend. Save!

A $3,000 credit card balance with a minimum payment of $62.35/month at 17.15% will take six years and ten months to pay off. And this is without any additional purchases. And the purchased item has long been used up.

Credit cards are the source of many financial disasters. Do not use a credit card unless you know what you are doing!

How to Pay Off Your Credit Card Balance

Step 1: **Make a list** of all the money you owe, starting with the highest interest rate. Include personal debt (money borrowed from family and friends). If you are late with any of these payments, call now and tell them why. Don't be embarrassed. You are just in debt. That does not make you a bad person. Here's how to start your list:

Who you owe   Balance owed   Interest rate   Minimum payment

Step 2: Try to get **lower interest rates** from your current credit cards. Call the highest interest rate credit card. Tell them you are considering switching to a card with a better rate, and ask them to meet the lower rate.

Step 3: **Start paying as much as you can**. The amount must be more than the total of the minimum monthly payments from above. Put the difference between the total minimums and the amount you can pay toward the credit card charging the highest interest rate. Once this credit card is paid off, call and close the account. Now start over again by paying off the remaining debt of the card with the highest rate. Include the total amount from the previous card plus more.

Step 4: **Learn from this problem**. Admit your mistake. Resolve not to make this mistake again.

Want to Improve Your Credit Score?

As a Money Coach and financial adviser, I urge each and every person to work diligently to improve his/her individual credit score. Your credit score is one of your most important possessions.

You must realize there are different sources for a credit score and some use different scales. The premier score is the FICO score, a proprietary product from a company called Fair Isaac and Company. The score ranges from 300 to 850.

Step 1 is to **check your credit reports for errors** at each of the three credit bureaus. Order your yearly credit reports for free through the official website sponsored by the three credit bureaus (www.annualcreditreport.com) or call 877-322-8228. I check one bureau every four months. Many reports contain errors, and 5% of consumers have serious errors that could result in less-favorable loan terms.

Next, **find out your score** so you can establish a baseline to measure progress in improving your score. I use CreditKarma.com, but be careful not to sign up for something that costs money, such as credit-monitoring services. CreditKarma also provides advice on how to help your score.

To **improve your score**, you must know how the score is calculated. Score components include the following:

☐ Payment history (35%)—whether you pay your bills on time.
☐ Debt levels (30%)—your balance versus the total amount of credit.
☐ Credit history (15%)—how long you have had credit.
☐ New debt (10%)—new credit applications.
☐ Credit mix (10%)—how much credit you have, the types of debt you have incurred. The "right" number of credit lines is five or six. Examples are student loan, home loan, car loan, and a couple of credit cards.

Here are some **hints**:

☐ Don't use a credit card if you cannot pay off the balance each month.

☐ If you use a credit card, use only one or a maximum of two cards.
☐ Don't use your credit card as an emergency fund.
☐ Pay off debt rather than move it around.
☐ It is better to have a little balance on a line of credit than have no balance at all.

Avoid "hard" inquiries by making sure your credit is checked only when you actually plan to use it. Example: when you test-drive a car, ask that your credit not be checked.

Finally, the Money Coach says you should have your own line of credit. Don't, for example, be just on your spouse's credit card. Get your own credit. But don't abuse it!

Declare Bankruptcy? Probably Not!

The bankruptcy question is one I frequently hear. My answer in nine out of ten situations is "No, it would not help you to declare bankruptcy!" As in all cases, when a substantial sum of money (as in bankruptcy) is thrown against a money problem, you will be short of funds again usually within two years unless the cause of the problem is addressed and solved.

Start by admitting that you have a problem and then solving the problem or, more likely, the problems:

Problem: **overspending**. Most people who spend too much know very well they spend more than they should. Solution: spend no more than you make; change your spending habits. It is your income that determines how much you can spend.

Problem: **"Where did the money go?"** Not being able to account for your money is a common problem. Most cannot figure out where 25%–40% of their take-home pay goes. Solution: write every expenditure down, and that means every dollar.

Problem: **"Not a clue."** I had a young couple visit me. Their issue was "Should we declare bankruptcy?" Each came to my office with a huge Starbucks and a really big calorie-stuffed muffin. After talking to them for ten minutes, I was convinced they did not have a clue about any connection between the $20 worth of stuff they brought along and the fact they could not pay for car insurance next week. No one can help not-a-clue people until they wake up and fix their problems.

Problem: **"If only my debt would go away, everything would be okay."** This is a close relative to "not a clue." Hello, the debt is not going away. Think about how you got the debt. Acknowledge mistakes. Change the way you do things. Fix the problems.

Problem: **"I didn't cause this problem. Somebody else did."** Sure, it was the economy, the administration, the mortgage company, the spouse, the boss, bad luck, etc. Solution: get real; it's the guy or gal you see in the mirror.

Problem: **"I lost my job or the car broke down or something unexpected happened, and I had to buy things with my credit**

card." Sorry, but the fact you did not have an emergency fund to draw upon during a crisis is not an uncontrolled, outside factor. Solution: start an emergency fund. The lack of one is your fault.

Problem: **spending nine dollars a gallon on gas and seven dollars a pound on tomatoes.** Nobody in his/her right mind would spend nine dollars a gallon for gas, right? Wrong, those who put consumable items on a credit card and make the minimum payments do. Just add 20–30% annual interest each month to the three dollars a gallon of gas and see what happens. It takes six to seven years to pay off purchases like this, and remember, by then, the tomatoes and the gas are long gone. Solution: pay off your credit card balance in full at the end of each month. It goes without saying that anyone contemplating bankruptcy should not be using credit cards for any purchase.

Final problem: **not taking responsibility for your own personal financial life.** Solution: Declare a PFC (personal financial crisis). Go on a war footing. Identify the problem. Change. Fix the issue.

On the income front, consider a second or third job; sell stuff you don't need (garage sale or eBay). Sell items of value you'd like to keep but can't afford (jewelry, coin collections, antique furniture, other collectables).

On the expense side, go on a beans-and-rice diet. Toss cable and internet. Downsize your residence. Sell one or both cars and use the bus. Stop buying clothes or eating out or paying for movies. You must spend only on the essentials: food, shelter, transportation. You must cut back on everything: turn off the lights, use less water (and of course no bottled water), raise the deductible on your insurance, brainstorm with your spouse and kids on how to save a dollar here and a dollar there.

Once you have an idea of how much money is available each month to pay down existing debt, put together a plan. Make paying off your debt the priority of your life.

Finally, when contemplating bankruptcy, consider that you are the one who borrowed the money and you have a legal and moral obligation to pay it back. Bankruptcy might lessen the legal obligation, but your moral duty remains. And a bankruptcy will always be with you. It may fall off your credit report in a decade or so, but for the rest of your life, a lender may ask, "Have you ever declared bankruptcy?" and you will have to answer yes.

So do everything you can to make sure that when a lender asks you this question, you can confidently say, "No!"

CHAPTER 5

Money Buddies and Money Success Stories

Money Habits of Your Peers

I'm Twenty and in Control of My Money Life

Money Advice from a Twenty-Nine-Year-Old

I'm Twenty-Seven; My Goal = Save $30,000 a Year

Have Fun without Spending a Lot of Money

Surround
yourself with
people
who have
good money
habits!

The more we do
for others,
the better
we are!

Money Habits of Your Peers

One of your goals should be to learn from others. Here are some money ideas to ponder from your peers.

Melissa is nineteen and has recently started college. She lists her money successes and failures like this:

Successes
- ☐ Putting money into a savings account
- ☐ Keeping receipts
- ☐ Allowing myself to only buy one thing when I go shopping for fun
- ☐ Doing my job well to get tips at work
- ☐ Bringing my brother and neighbors to school in exchange for gas money

Failures
- ☐ Buying things from unreliable websites online
- ☐ Buying clothes online that I don't know will fit

Kaitlyn is twenty-one and attends a university in South Africa; she wants to be an accountant.

> I like the idea of saving 10% of your income because it gives me an achievable goal. But I would like to give myself a 2% leeway, because there are those months where necessary additional expenses come up. I worry that when someone saves less that the 10% goal, he/she might become very discouraged and quit saving all together. I want the saver to continue saving even though the goal was missed. I'd rather be in the orange zone instead of the red zone. I want to keep on saving no matter what!

Emily is twenty-three and working hard for the future. Here's what got her started in the right money direction:

> Having a 50% minimum savings rule has worked well for me. When I started working at 16, I started saving 50% of every paycheck I received and put that money in a separate savings account I never touched. The remainder of my paychecks would be used to pay for my car insurance, gas, and phone bill. Anything left over, I would put into the savings account or use as some spending money to go to the movies with my friends or buy a new outfit. I also didn't touch or consider credit cards until my first year of college, and then I applied for a credit card through my bank with a $500 limit. I specified its purpose to be used for gas only. That way I could begin building credit without the temptation to purchase more than I really needed. Emily, who lives at home, now saves 75% of her paycheck. Goals include a new car and a place of her own.

Megan is twenty-seven and is well into her career. Here are her money tips:

> Buy a large jar and start putting your change inside. Hundreds of dollars are lost by not saving change and converting it later into dollars using machines at local grocery stores or banks.
>
> Find free local seminars in your area and attend to learn more tips. Ask questions.
>
> Instead of having a lot of money put away into a savings account, consider investing in a mutual fund or Exchange Traded Fund which provides a larger return.

Make your money work for you, invest it wisely and expand your portfolio.

Always have a slush fund of liquid cash available in times of need.

I'm Twenty and in Control of My Money Life

"More or less in control," says twenty-year-old Jessica, who has run a coaching business out of her home for three years. Jessica has been married to John for over three years, and they have a little three-year-old girl. As a Money Coach, I was impressed with Jessica's approach to family finances. In her own words:

> It's mostly common sense: You can't spend more than you make! You must save in order to live! After graduating from high school, I married John who by then had been in the work force for a year. I must admit I was a bit [okay, a lot] taken back by John's spending habits. I sort of [actually, with emphasis] put my foot down. I told him he had to get it together [I used different words actually]. We now talk about money a couple of times a week, and the conversations are much less confrontational after years of practice.
>
> We don't use credit cards anymore. At first we [he] did overspend using those cards. It was a real eye opener. Now I look at both of our bank accounts each day either on my phone or on my computer. There will be no overspending! I do have a written budget, and it is pretty tight. For example, we grocery shop once a week with a budget of $50. As we shop I put down the price of each item on my calculator. Once we reach $50, we stop and check out. Clothes and shoes are in the "fun" category, and we indulge once a year. Our debit cards are set to decline if we pass the amount in our bank account.
>
> We have gotten over the "spend it because it is there" mentality. We have an emergency fund which would carry us through two months on no

income. I am building this account, hoping we never have to use it. We are saving for a house by paying rent to his parents.

My advice to others is learn from your mistakes and never make that mistake again. Our big mistake was to buy our first car at $19,000 with a 21% interest rate. The plan was to double the principle payments each month. But then John got fewer hours and his monthly income dropped by $1000. Then he lost that job. We did not think about "life happening." Now we have a car worth $7000 and we owe $15,000. And we bought the first car we saw. We should have looked at other, less expensive, vehicles. In addition, I tell everyone even if you can afford it, don't overspend. Save your money for your future.

Money Coach comment: Good job, Jessica! You are on the right track. Keep moving forward. My advice to young professionals is to exchange money ideas with your peers. Jessica would be the perfect budget buddy.

Money Advice from a Twenty-Nine-Year-Old

Rachel is a money success at twenty-nine. I asked her to give some advice for those in their twenties:

> Start saving for your retirement now, even in small amounts. Do not leave that for your thirties.
>
> Don't make decisions based on the assumption that your parents will bail you out when you run into financial troubles. Own your money and financial decisions every step of the way starting with your very first job.
>
> Just because all of your friends are buying a house doesn't necessarily mean you should. Do careful research, and make that decision based on what is right for you.
>
> Your twenties are a time when you create habits which will stay with you for the rest of your life—both good and bad. The habits you create now can set you up for a healthy financial future for the rest of your life. Create a budget, and stick with it. Pay your credit cards off fully every month.
>
> Don't be afraid to ask questions! If you don't know about something, reach out to a trusted adviser and ask. Learn as much as possible about what your options are.
>
> Health savings account plans can be very helpful since they are tax-free; ask your employer if they offer that option.
>
> Create both short-term and long-term financial goals. Write them down.
>
> Include some discretionary funds into your budget so when those once-in-a-lifetime adventures come your way, you can say yes!

Hats off to Rachel. She has done a good job with her money and is well on the way to a successful money life.

Be like Rachel!

I'm Twenty-Seven; My Goal = Save $30,000 a Year

Alicia was an independent contractor at a beauty salon; she paid monthly rent for her chair. She had been working (and saving) since age thirteen. Her advice to others at that time was: "Sacrifice. Don't give in to temptations, to luxuries while you are young." My Money Coach advice to guys: "Marry someone like Alicia."

Alicia is now twenty-seven. Six years ago, Brad took my advice and married her; they now have two children and own their second house. She also owns a beauty salon, works full-time as a beautician, and rents out five chairs to others. She mentioned that four years ago, the family goal was to save $30,000 a year. I asked, "How in the world did you do that?" These are her own words:

> My father taught me, always, always save. Back before I got married to Brad, I put my savings into three places: buy a house bucket; emergency fund; spare change in my spoil me account.
>
> After we married, we put our money together. I took the lead in managing our family finances. I pay the bills, keep track of expenses, and generally I am the money person under our roof. Brad is okay with money, but he tends to be more the spender than the saver. We talk about money frequently. I admit I usually initiate "the talk." Brad and I are usually on the same page, but I hold the page and give gentle direction. Each January, we review our financial world. Together we review the previous year's expenses and set goals on where to cut back on spending. We always find our money is being spent on things we really don't need like eating out and entertainment.
>
> Early in our marriage Brad and I bought a small house. We had saved the down payment, which was only $10,000 because we got a VA

loan. But with baby number 2 due, we knew we needed a larger house. Our initial goal was to save all Brad's salary and pay all the bills with my income. That was too much of a challenge, so we settled on saving $2,500 a month, $30,000 a year. But because I was growing my business, our average savings was only $2,000/month.

Brad was on board with our savings plan. I suggested he take the Dave Ramsey course, but he was very busy at work and there was "never enough time"—it never happened. What did happen was he read an article about how to pay off debt. Start with the smallest debt first, then with the extra money from these payments plus the budgeted amount for the second debt he was able to pay that off. Soon, all his debt was greatly reduced, and the savings bug took control of his thinking about family finances.

Three years ago, we paid off our joint out-standing debt. My grandmother left me enough to pay off $15,000 in student debt, and together we tackled Brad's vehicle loans [he collects motorcycles].

I put family savings in several different accounts. That way we don't see the total savings and are less tempted to spend money on things we really don't need. We have a single joint check-ing and savings account. Brad's income goes here, and we pay all our personal bills from checking and put what is left in savings.

When I bought my own salon two years ago, the start-up costs added up quickly. My business income goes into two accounts and each account has a checking and savings component. One is my personal account and other covers business expenses. I wait until the end of the year to pay myself wages. That's so I won't spend it.

I talk to both kids, even the three-year old, all the time about money. I emphasize what things cost and the difference between needs and wants. I point out the fact that it costs money to replace things so when something is broken during a tantrum, that toy is not replaced. This is a lesson in life for the kids.

The future—across all our accounts, our family currently saves about $4,200 a month.

Money Coach comment: With $50,400 a year savings, hats off to Alicia and Brad—and the kids!

Read more about Alicia when she was younger in "Savings 101: She's Twenty and Saves $500 a Month."

Have Fun without Spending a Lot of Money

Money buddy Rachel, twenty-nine and exploring her third career, shares ideas about having fun without breaking the bank:

> A common theme for today's young adults is the hesitancy to go against the grain. Most spend all of what they bring in (and more), and since most social things revolve around spending money, they are building debt instead of saving for the future.
>
> Prioritize entertainment choices so you don't feel the need to say yes to everything.
>
> My generation spends a lot of money on alcohol. Only bring cash with you to a bar so you can limit how much you spend on drinks. The mark up on alcohol is astronomical. Also, try to plan these meet-ups during happy hour when drinks [and food] are considerably cheaper. Or consider hanging out at someone's house instead of a bar so you can buy the alcohol from a liquor store at a much lower rate.
>
> Get the cheap seats at events like Rock Pile tickets for Rockies games. Get all of the ambiance of the ballpark at a fraction of the price.
>
> Google free things to do [in your city] this weekend.
>
> Get out and explore nature. Ride a bike. Instead of a movie with popcorn, take a hike and have a picnic.
>
> Don't feel like you have to spend a lot of money on dates. Often, the thought and planning behind a date means more than the dollar amount you spend. Go Dutch. Cook at home.

Rachel has the right idea. It is best to practice frugality early in your career. Spending less then becomes a habit and saves you money for decades.

Don't forget your local library. You can go to your library and get books, books on CD, and movies. With your library card, you also can watch free movies on your computer via Kanopy. You can download free books and audio books via Overdrive as well as free audio books via Libby.

Check out free museum days and many other educational and fun things you can do in your area.

Exchange ideas with your friends. Organize fun things together.

Remember, your date will be attracted to you if you have money sense. Think big. Think frugal!

CHAPTER 6

Education and Student Debt

Education and Your Career

How to Get a Job

Paying for Higher Education

Stories of Students and Debt

Save early
and
often!

Ever dollar saved
or invested
needs a purpose
written on it!

Education and Your Career

Secrets of Life

Secret to making money = getting a job.
Secret to getting a job = education and attitude.
Secret to education = showing up for class, studying hard, pursuing courses that will lead to "your" job, graduating on time.

Education

Education 1: formal education, K–12, trade school, college or university.
Education 2: informal education, how to deal with people, verbal and written presentation skills, how to be an employee or how to be a boss, how to be a team player.

Attitude

You can be the best-educated person in your class, but you will fail if you don't have the right attitude.

Paying for Education

Gathering sufficient funds starts early. Saving for college by your family should start at birth. Your contribution to your own college fund should start in elementary or middle school. The harder you study and the more you know, the better chance for "free" money: scholarships, grants, and the like. Pick an educational institute you can afford. Your goal is to graduate and get a job without any debt. It is often not possible to have saved enough before trade school or college. This brings on student debt. If you must take on debt, then select a course of study that will lead to a job so you can pay off the debt in one to two years (three years at the most).

What Not to Do

Do not waste your time (and money). Apply yourself 100% to the task at hand.

Self-motivation is key. Just do it!

I've seen many who spend $10,000 on a certificate course and then do not take the job as a certified nursing assistant, for example. Loan repayments start. Debtors discover payments for past classes are deferred when they are enrolled in another course. So they spend $10,000 to be a dental assistant. And then they don't want that job. Soon, they are in their thirties with $40,000 in student debt—and no job. Don't let this happen to you.

Remember

Only about one in four graduates end up working in their declared major. You probably will have multiple jobs in your forty-plus years of work life, most of which you will not be able to predict when you graduate. Take courses that are applicable outside your major. Your Money Coach is in career number 6. I had no idea!

How to Get a Job

As you know, the secret to making money is going to work. Your best investment is education—formal education plus street smarts. Whether you are in school or not in school, learn as much as you can about as many things as you can. I recall going to a high school class reunion where our group was hosted by soon-to-be-graduating seniors. I thought back to my own graduation day and concluded these kids, like me then, had no idea what their work life would be like in the decades ahead. I am in my sixth career, and that does not count being a bellhop, a lifeguard, a KFC french fry guy, and a funeral home helper.

Bottom line: Learn everything you can. You are going to need that knowledge. Your experience is everything you have done. Flaunt it!

I highly recommend to all high school, trade school, and college graduates the book entitled *Designing Your Life* by Bill Burnett and Dave Evans. Here are some facts from *Designing Your Life*:

> In the United States, only 27% of college grads end up in a career related to their majors. I majored in History and never held a history-major-related job, but it was the broad-based Liberal Arts education which did me well.
>
> In the United States, only 20 percent of all the jobs available are posted on the internet or anywhere else. Do not get caught up believing the internet is the end all place to look for a job.
>
> Internet job descriptions are not usually written by the hiring manager nor does the job description capture what the job requires for success.

So how will you find a job? It will not be just by looking on the internet. It most probably will be through someone you know from your network of contacts. My own network in high school was my mom; she got me all my teen jobs. Your goal is to build your network, to meet as many people as possible. Overcome your shyness. Ask for informational interviews, meetings that are separate from the actual job search. Ask for advice and guidance; see if you can find a mentor. Volunteer. Look for internships, paid or unpaid. Work part-time. Knock on doors. Visit local businesses. Don't be afraid to ask. My second career happened because I walked into the government agency after receiving a rejection letter.

Seek help. In Colorado Springs, we have the Pikes Peak Workforce Center, which holds many how-to-get-a-job workshops. Check out what's available in your city.

Improve your interpersonal skills. Be able to write understandable sentences without spelling and grammar mistakes. Start practicing with your posts and your texts. Never ever quit a job by "ghosting" (walking out and not telling anyone).

What can employers check? Employers can check an employment screening credit report (not score). Have good credit. Prospective companies check your social sites. Be careful what you post.

Work on your interview skills. Don't take your mother to the interview (has happened). Always show up for an interview. Turn off electronic devices. Give a firm handshake. Make eye contact. Study the company before the visit. Have a tailored résumé. Ask questions. Attitude is all-important ("I believe I have the skills and motivation to help your company"). Reliability is key ("Yes, I have a car. My kids can get to and from school. I have a watch and can tell the time"). Look for a job offer rather than a job. Both you and the company want a fit.

Look in the mirror. Your job search focus starts with yourself. What is your motivation? What is your passion? Enthusiasm is the key to success in everything you do. What are your qualifications? How can you help the company you are interviewing? Remember "interviewing" is a two-way street. How can that company help you advance your own life goals? Practice your writing skills, your verbal skills, your teamwork skills. Demonstrate a great work ethic. Show **enthusiasm**!

Paying for Higher Education

One of the most challenging goals in life is paying for your education. Best, of course, is to have saved the money ahead of time and having someone else pay part of your education through family contributions and scholarships and grants. Most students, however, will have to borrow money. And when you borrow money, you must pay it back. Your goal should be to build a college fund ahead of time and to pay any and all borrowed money back in one, two, or three years max. Set a limit on how much you borrow. How to do this?

Parents, grandparents, other relatives, and friends should be encouraged to contribute to a 529 college savings plan. Each state has its own plan, but you can put money in any state plan. I recommend Utah (https://my529.org). This money is invested and is not taxed when used for approved educational purposes. Invest for the long term; a good idea is to use age-related investment choices, which are aggressive when the kids are young and more conservative as college age approaches.

A great way to prepare for college is to do well in K–12. Study hard, volunteer often, work as much as you can without interfering with your studies. It is your life, and you must do the best you can before college or trade school. Focus not on your first job after graduation; focus on a career and what contribution you want to make to society.

As a junior in high school, start learning about scholarships and grants and student loans. The options are many, often confusing, and constantly changing. Talk to a counsellor in your high school and, if possible, a college-level counsellor.

Learn to manage your money at a young age. Most successful twenty- and thirty-year-olds start working part-time jobs in their early teens. Then they start budgeting and saving part of the money they earn. They cut back on wants, and they focus on their future—college and a career.

While still in high school or before your next year in an institution of higher learning, check out the Free Application for Federal Student Aid (FAFSA). You may qualify for up to $30,000 in aid. Many families skip this step because they think they make too much money. If your family makes less than $250,000 a year, apply. You will need your tax returns, your own bank/investment balances, and the names of the schools to which you are applying.

Look for work while attending school. Most schools have an employment website.

Not everyone needs four years at a university. Attend the local community college for your first two years. Just make sure your courses are transferable to your university of choice. Or pursue a trade (welders can make $140,000 a year). Work should be enjoyable; never work for long in a job that's bad for you.

Explore going to a university in another country. It is often less expensive (most foreign schools are publicly funded), and the foreign cultural experience is priceless.

Check out federal tax credits, such as American Opportunity and Lifetime Learning Credits, when budgeting for college.

Search for scholarships with books and apps (Scholly app for Apple products, for example).

High school seniors should investigate areas where a potential job is in strong demand (healthcare, teachers). In some critical areas, your debt is forgiven after you work for so many years. This also is true when working for the betterment of society (as in the Peace Corps or AmeriCorps).

Some employers contribute to employee education. Be sure to include this question when you interview with companies of interest. Here is a short list: Sotheby's, Abbott, Aeta, Millennium Trust Co., Penguin Random House, Hewlett Packard, Options Clearing Corporation, Carvana, Andersen Tax, Honeywell, Starbucks.

The state of Maine has a program for residents called the educational opportunity tax credit. The amount you must pay for student loans is credited against your annual state income tax.

MOOCs, or massive open online courses, are free online courses. Check to see if the course provides credits toward a degree. Online courses can be paid with 529 monies only if they are sponsored by an accredited college that the student is enrolled in.

Don't forget to live below your means while in school. A pizza a week for four years could cost you thousands in student debt. Live at home if that works for you. Call it cohousing, and establish guidelines with your parents to differentiate between being a kid and being a student attending an institute of higher education.

Graduate! Don't waste time and money by taking course after course and then dropping out. To win, you must graduate.

A list of online resources for paying for higher education is available in the Resources section of this book. Paying for education will take a lot of research, but the end result is well worth the effort.

Stories of Students and Debt

Following are real-life stories of how students have approached paying for college or trade school.

Hannah and Bart are sister and brother, ages eighteen and sixteen. Hannah is a freshman in college; Bart is a junior in high school. In high school, both were/are involved in the Pathways program (often called concurrent enrollment), whereby they take college credit classes as part of their high school schedule. Hannah graduated with both her high school diploma and an AA degree in general studies. Bart, as a junior, already has sufficient credits for a high school diploma, but he will continue the current year and the next year in high school to obtain additional college credit. When attending high school, the college courses are free, a unique opportunity to take college courses at no cost. Hannah, whose grades put her second in her high school class, is attending college on a full scholarship, which also offers part-time employment as part of the package. These students are working hard to "pay" for college via free courses and scholarships. Follow their example!

Nicole, age twenty-one, is a senior at a state university. She will graduate with no debt. The reason: her parents raised her to pay for things on her own. She started working at fifteen. Her school expenses, therefore, are paid by working. She is a full-time student and works approximate twenty-five hours per week; she also works all summer. "It was difficult at first, but the end goal of a degree with no debt is definitely worth the sacrifice." Nicole chose a lower-cost university; she estimates her total expenditures for four years of tuition, books, gas, food, and parking at $25,000–$26,000. She lives with her parents. Her degree, human services, requires two part-time internships (note: internships are often paid). She gets good grades but has no scholarship or grants. Nicole has self-discipline; she tracks her expenses and puts money aside for school at every opportunity.

Melissa, age nineteen, has just started a two-year degree program in photography. She will graduate with no debt. The reason: paying for college is a joint effort of Melissa, her parents, and her grandmother. Melissa is paying for phone and TV, clothes, personal

items, eating out, and miscellaneous purchases. Her parents are paying for gas and insurance for the car, essential living expenses, and
airfare home for Christmas. Grandma started a 529 college savings
plan for Melissa fifteen years ago, and the accumulated money will
pay for tuition and room and board. Cost estimates for each year in
these categories is $27,000. The 529 money should pay for most of
the two years. Melissa also has a part-time job with a photography
studio.

Stacey, age nineteen, is a sophomore attending two expensive universities. She just acquired a research position with data
science and is interested in cybersecurity. A university degree will
cost $75,000 per year. Her first year and a half has been a financial
struggle. "I am a struggling college student and kind of figuring it
all out as I go along." She has student loans and is working part-
time as a barista and as a researcher. But Stacey has a plan: she is
on track to receive a two-and-a-half-year scholarship from ROTC.
Once she passes the tests, she will be eligible for a full tuition scholarship, which includes tuition, room and board, $500 per semester
for books, and a monthly stipend. She will have a four-year military
commitment upon graduation. During her military service, she will
pay off her student debt balance. After her military commitment, she
plans to use the GI bill for a master's degree. Search the Summary of
VA Education Benefits document.

Liz and Christopher, both age thirty, are married and have
one child. Christopher currently has $36,000 in student debt from a
master's degree (original debt level: $40,000). Liz has an AA degree
with no student debt. She has used a Pell Grant (single mom), parental help, and money from working multiple jobs. Liz recommends
single moms check with the local Social Services Department. She
learned from them of the Pell Grant and was able to get day-care
vouchers to take care of her son while she attended classes. Liz and
Christopher have put together an aggressive plan to pay down debt.
They have cut back on family expenses, and they use actual paper
envelopes as part of family budgeting. After absolute essentials are
paid each month, all remaining funds go to extra principal on credit
card debt. Once a card is paid off, the money in the budget for that

card is applied to the next card. Christopher's monthly student debt payment now is about $500. Soon, when the credit cards are paid off, the family will be able to apply an additional $1,000 per month to his student debt. Their son, noting the example of his parents, began saving part of his money for college at age seven.

Erin, age twenty-three, is married to a soldier. She works "full-time," but her employer often shuts down a day or two each week, giving her less-than-anticipated salary. When her husband is deployed in the coming months, Erin plans to work part-time for Starbucks. Starbucks' employees who work twenty hours plus a week receive assistance to pay concurrent schooling. She will use the money for an online course to complete her AA degree in early childhood education. Erin also will use her small stipend as the spouse of a soldier.

Tyler, a married millennial who conducts a seminar entitled How to Attract Millennials, notes that different things are important to different people. Home ownership is not on his list, yet. Ben's priority was to pay off $20,000 in student debt; he did it in ten months. Now his priority is saving for the education of his two kids. Ben's family occupies a basement apartment in the home of his wife's parents. It's called cohousing. Won't work for everyone, but it definitely is worth exploring.

Have an education plan well before you leave high school. And work very hard to pay down any student debt within a few years of your degree or certificate.

CHAPTER 7

Life

Okay, You've Started Your First Real Job; Now What?

What Is Your Money Score?

Side Hustle: Multiple Sources of Income

Desperate in Des Moines

When My Dad Was Laid Off

Hit-by-a-Truck Planning for Young Adults

It's not the lack of resources.

It's the lack of resourcefulness!

Okay, You've Started Your First Real Job; Now What?

Starting your first job or moving on to a new career is a critical point in your life and your money life. The focus must now be on postponing instant gratification and planning a full, useful, and interesting life. Spend some time focusing on your future and on your legacy. Your legacy is what you pass on to your descendants as well as your personal contribution to all mankind in the future. Your legacy to your family is your monetary possessions, but more importantly, it is your values, your accomplishments, your dreams. Your degree of success will depend in large part on how you manage your money.

Let this be your starting point. Understand where your money goes now (track expenses), and then decide if this is the best use of your money for the future. Spend wisely and start saving for specific goals in the near term (foreign travel) as well as the distant future (retirement). It's your money, your future. Take control!

Alexis, thirty-seven, is not happy that she and her best friend did not save money when they worked together in their twenties. At age twenty-five, they each were bringing in $60,000 a year and had few financial obligations. Alexis and her friend spent all their money and more on things that now seem irresponsible.

Brooke, twenty-nine, will soon continue her career as a behavioral counsellor in a new state. The first few months will be part-time. Her plan is to develop a budget and live within her means on the initial lower salary. Then when she becomes full-time, she will put the "extra" money aside for her dream house.

When you are at a crossroads in life, the direction you take is up to you. Please choose the path that is best for you!

What Is Your Money Score?

Answer these fifteen questions, and learn how you are handling your money. Tally your score at the end. Find your grade. Then work to improve your money score.

1. Financial goals (10 points max) _____
   - ☐ I have financial goals that are precise, achievable, have a timeline, and are written down. (10 points)
   - ☐ I have financial goals in my head, but they are not written down. (5 points)
   - ☐ I have no financial goals. (0 points)

2. Money talk (10 points max) _____
   - ☐ I have regular money talks at least once a month with my partner. (10 points)
   - ☐ I don't have a partner, but I do talk about my finances with others. (8 points)
   - ☐ I think talking about my money is a good idea and will start discussions with my partner, or I will seek a budget buddy or a savings buddy and exchange ideas on a regular basis. (7 points)

3. Living within your means (10 points max) _____
   - ☐ I know for sure that I live within my means; I have more money coming in than going out. (10 points)
   - ☐ I think I live within my means. (4 points)
   - ☐ I am struggling financially but understand I am responsible for my finances and am working hard to balance my budget. (5 points)
   - ☐ I just don't know. (0 points)

4. Tracking expenses and budgeting (–5 to +10 points) _____
   - ☐ I keep track of all my expenses and use this information to make a budget with specific maximum amounts in each spending category. (10 points)
   - ☐ I know roughly how much I spend. (5 points)

- ☐ All I know is that there is no money left over at the end of the month. (0 points)
- ☐ I don't even try to keep track of expenses. (–5 points)

5. Emergency fund (–5 to +10 points) _____
    - ☐ I have what I think is an adequate emergency fund, money set aside for expenses that are not in the budget. (10 points)
    - ☐ I have some money set aside for emergencies, but not enough. (5 points)
    - ☐ I do not have an emergency fund. (–5 points)

6. Savings and investment plan (10 points max) _____
    - ☐ I have both savings and investments. (8 points)
    - ☐ I know the asset allocation of my investments. (1 point)
    - ☐ I know the annual expense percentage of my investments. (1 point)

7. Manage your investments (10 points max) _____
    - ☐ I have investments, and I manage them myself. (8 points)
    - ☐ I know not to buy a financial product recommended by someone who makes a commission on the sale. (2 points)
    - ☐ I let someone else handle my investments. (–3 points)
    - ☐ I don't have anything invested for the future. (–5 points)

8. Insurance (10 points max) _____
    - ☐ I have health insurance for myself and family. (5 points)
    - ☐ I have life insurance if I have anyone who depends on me. (2 points)
    - ☐ I have auto insurance. (1 point)
    - ☐ I have homeowner's or rental insurance. (1 point)
    - ☐ I have umbrella insurance (extra liability). (1 point)

9. Credit cards (–5 to +10 points) _____
    - ☐ I use a credit card and always pay off my balance each month. (10 points)

☐ I do not pay my credit card off each month. (–5 points)

☐ I do not use a credit card. (10 points)

10. Credit management (10 points max) _____

☐ I have reviewed my credit reports in the past year at AnnualCreditReport.com or will do so within two days. (5 points)

☐ I know my credit score or will check CreditKarma.com within two days. (5 points)

☐ I have no idea about credit reports or credit scores. (0 points)

11. Bank fees, including monthly, ATM, overdraft fees (10 points max) _____

☐ I have an account but do not pay bank fees. (10 points)

☐ Each month, I have some bank fees. (0 points)

☐ Occasionally, I pay a bank fee; each time I learn never to do that again. (8 points)

☐ I don't use a bank. I use payday lending. (–5 points)

12. Debt management (10 points max) _____

☐ I know exactly how much money I owe, to whom, and how much. (5 points)

☐ I am paying my debt payments regularly. (5 points)

☐ I have outstanding debts that I cannot pay. (–5 points)

13. Windfall of cash like a tax refund and others (–5 to +10 points) _____

☐ I understand the concept that I should not use a windfall of cash to pay off a money problem (example: overspending) without first solving the problem. (10 points)

☐ If I get money, I spend it right away. (–5 points).

14. Financial literacy (10 points max) _____

☐ I know the benefits of I-Bonds and Roth IRAs. (10 points)

□ I plan to learn the benefits of I-Bonds and Roth IRAs in the next week. (8 points)

□ What are I-Bonds and Roth IRAs? (0 points)

15. Hit-by-a-truck plan (10 points max) _____

□ I have an updated will and have reviewed how all my property transfers to my beneficiaries—payable on death and my beneficiaries. (8 points)

□ I have a survivor file, and my survivors know where it is. (2 points)

Total score _____
Grades
  A+   over 120
  A   95–119
  B   80–94
  C   50–79
  D   21–49
  Fail 20 and below

Side Hustle: Multiple Sources of Income

For many young professionals, gone are the days of only having traditional nine-to-five, Monday-to-Friday employment. Side hustle is a way to make extra cash that provides funding for things you really want to do or, in many cases, to survive. The key words are "flexible" (time) and "extra" (cash).

Let me introduce Abigail, the side-hustle queen. Abigail is twenty-eight, a single mom, works full-time, and attends grad school. She has worked or is working side-hustle jobs just to pay the bills. She lives in a town where the median household income is $90,000 and the living wage is $31 an hour. Abigail makes $45,000 a year, and her salary as a librarian is $24 an hour. Fortunately, through a friend, she has a lower-than-average payment for an apartment. Her child support goes to day-care costs. Abigail's budget is tight, but she manages by working extremely hard, improvising, and hustling other sources of income.

Here are some of Abigail's side hustles over the past four years:

☐ **Indeed.com.** Abigail found a job quickly on this site. She collected retail data for marketing intelligence for retail stores such as Walmart and Target. She made $600–$800 a month. She was able to take her son with her because it was similar to a "secret shopper" position. During this period, she was working on her Bachelor of Science degree.

☐ **Painting business.** Using her artistic side, Abigail painted sayings on wood tree slices and advertised her work on Facebook.

☐ **Baby clothes.** Abigail went to thrift stores and bought high-end brands that had been donated. She then flipped the pieces online. She followed mom groups online to keep abreast of the trends. Once, she bought a Stella McCartney baby jacket on eBay for $300 (asking $450), joined a group of moms with expensive tastes, and rented out the jacket on weekends. She made $400 renting the jacket and eventually sold it for $250. That was plus $450.

☐ **Group studies.** She was contacted because of her LinkedIn profile to order anything off the McDonald's menu online from their app. That was $75.

☐ **Boutique business.** Abigail took out a $5,000 loan and was able to pay it back within two months. She made a profit of $15,000 on sales of $35,000.

☐ **Selling stuff.** Needing a baby sitter for the upcoming weekend, Abigail went through her closet and found clothes she seldom wore. She posted them online to a Buy, Sell, Trade group. That was $140.

Abigail is confident that once she has completed her master's, she will be able to land a higher-paying job in her field. She hopes to be able to purchase a home soon. She will use her tax refund to get ahead on car payments and pay off the car sooner. When she is finished with school, she wants to open an online boutique again but without going through a middleman like she did last time. She will buy directly from the vendors. "I have a lot of ideas for the future, but I take comfort in knowing that as life often doesn't go the way we hope or expect it to, if we are creative and determined, we can make any situation work." Way to go Abigail!

Alexi, thirty-seven, is a side-hustle princess. She has four jobs, all of which provide necessary contributions to the family income (she is married and has a third grader and a big excitable dog named Murkwood). Alexi is one test short of a bachelor's degree and is currently taking prerequisites for a radiological technician program. Her medical AA degree will take two to three years to complete. She plans to work in the medical field as her full-time job (flexible three 12-hour shifts per week). At present, her major income-producing job is twenty-five hours per week at a restaurant (where she knows the owner). She supports her husband by working ten hours at a sports outlet, working substitute shifts at a large hotel (with a retirement plan with 6% matching), and cleaning houses when she needs a little extra. Currently, she balances all four jobs so she'll have time to spend with her family. When Alexi starts full-time on the medical AA degree next year, she will rebalance her work schedule to fit her roles of wife and mom and student. Alexi is working hard and knows where she is going. Good job!

More side hustle from my local "word of mouth" app:

- ☐ "I purchased my own travel agency and put into it as little or as much time as I choose. I do five to ten hours a week because I work full-time."
- ☐ "I donate plasma."
- ☐ "I work from home, setting up appointments and opening new shopping accounts for a large manufacturing company with an Amazon-type delivery service. I work from anywhere on my phone or laptop. No kids. No inventory. No quotas."
- ☐ "Network marketing. Direct sales."
- ☐ "I refer people to online stores, and if they end up shopping there, I get a bonus."

Google "side hustle." Check out (https://www.sidehustlenation. com). The ideas are endless: teach English and/or tutor, drive (Lyft or Uber), deliver (UberEats or Door Dash), cook, sell on Amazon or eBay, house-sit/pet-sit; hang out with strangers via RentaFriend.com.

My suggestion is to identify your skills/passions and figure out a way to make extra money while having fun. But make sure you have a definite, written goal for the extra money you earn.

Desperate in Des Moines

A desperate family writes a "We need help" email to me after reading one of my articles or viewing a TV segment. Unfortunately, it happens all too often. It is difficult to provide worthwhile advice when I have so little information, but I must try.

Today's story involves a family of four. The father is out of work; the mom's meager salary cannot support the family. They have $40,000 in credit card debt plus a mortgage and a home equity loan. Increasing debt, no savings, no emergency fund, no college fund—bleak circumstances, uncertain future, increasing stress. Help!

I am a financial adviser, a Money Coach. A coach educates and prepares someone for the race. If the runner starts the race without preparation and then falls out after a couple of laps, my coaching advice is to stop and start over and do it right. Unfortunately, this does not help this family in their situation. So I try to help.

This is my reply: "You have my sympathy for your situation. I'll try to provide what advice and support I can. There are two sides to family finances—income and outgo. You must work hard on both sides."

Income. Redouble your efforts to increase income. This possibly means getting a second job, looking for work in a different industry, and/or accepting part-time work. Use all resources, including friends/family, temp agencies, online job search sites, etc. If there is downtime, volunteer somewhere. Sell anything you don't need. Continue your attempts to downsize your living quarters; look at downsizing your vehicle(s).

Outgo. Declare a financial emergency and cut back in all areas. Don't use bottled water or eat out or buy the more expensive processed food or have cable TV. Track every dollar you spend. Most families don't know where 25–50% of their money goes. Once you know where the money goes, cut back in all areas. This is a family effort; include the kids.

Credit cards. Stop using all credit cards immediately, and use cash only. Call each card company and explain your situation and work out a payment plan. See a nonprofit credit counselor, such as Transformance, Transformanceusa.org, 1-800-249-2227.

Safety net. Every community has a safety net; find out how you can get help for food, shelter, transportation, and education.

Learn from your mistakes. Credit card debt, home equity loan, no emergency fund, overspending—once you get a positive cash flow, don't make any one of these financial mistakes again.

The answer is take control of your financial world before disaster happens!

MONEY SENSE FOR YOUNG PROFESSIONALS

When My Dad Was Laid Off

When Cindy lost her job a couple of years ago, her dad wrote her this letter:

Dear Cindy,
Twenty-five years ago I was called into the CEO's office and advised I was part of a "downsizing" effort by my company. There had been previous "reductions in force." I had known my time might be limited, and I made a half-hearted declaration to look around. But as a senior Program Director, I was caught up in the day-to-day effort to get things done. I was shocked. Suddenly I was unemployed.

I had a family of four to support, house payments to make, and two college funds requiring contributions. I had a lot going for me. Your mom immediately sought full time employment despite my suggestion that we wait for a few months. I had an emergency fund to cover bare bone expenses and a solid determination to survive and prosper. I immediately applied for unemployment although all my life I had considered unemployment to be "welfare," something to be avoided. When I learned I had contributed all my work life to an unemployment fund for this very contingency, the decision to apply became a no brainer. I checked COBRA and found I could continue health insurance for the family even though, at that time, it cost 103% of the combined contributions of myself and my former employer. Thank goodness, your mother quickly got a full time job with benefits.

To collect unemployment those days, you had to provide a list each week outlining what activities you undertook to find employment. You also had to spend volunteer hours helping at the work force center. I took the volunteer time seriously, made many contacts, and learned from others how to best use my time. Today, all these decades later, I visit our local work force center as a volunteer. The white board in the waiting room contained points on how to write a resume. Inside there were dozens of job seekers typing away on a large bank of computers. Classrooms were full of people learning the ins and outs of getting a job. My seminar will be on "How to Survive Financially After a Job Loss." I plan to give a second seminar on "How to Manage your Money once the New Paycheck Arrives."

At home where most of my job search efforts took place, I turned my occasional home office into "my office." My job now was to get a job, and this became my office. Every morning I would put on my business clothes and go to my office to "work." A job search environment is very important - it must be professional. Do not go to a corner of your bedroom in pajamas and think you are doing all you can to get a job. Go to your office and work hard at finding a job.

I talked to my friends, former co-workers, and contacts. Then I talked to friends of friends, friends of former co-workers, and friends of contacts. I asked for advice and guidance and help. I tried to get out of my "office" daily to meet people face-to-face.

Looking back, the experience of being unemployed added to my life experience.

Eventually, after much research, I decided to go into business for myself. I would sell advertising for several small publications. Commission only, but it worked. And it started me down a new, very exciting career path. The process took 6–7 months and was very stressful. I learned to exercise every day and to eat the right foods at mealtime only. I came away from this experience a better person. Unemployment led me to a better life.

Love, Dad

Cindy now says, "Thanks, Dad, you made me feel better, and yes, with much effort, my life did improve."

Hit-by-a-Truck Planning for Young Adults

Okay, you are in your twenties or thirties, and you are never going to die. But your parents and your grandparents and other relatives are going to leave this world one of these days. If you know the basics, you can help them. Remember, a Money Coach cannot provide legal advice.

The Will

Not everyone needs a will. If money accounts have an up-to-date "beneficiary" or "payable on death" designation, the account goes directly to the beneficiary—no need for a will. If assets have what is called a beneficiary title (house, car), no need for a will. If there is a list of those who will receive nontitled stuff (mementos, jewelry, etc.), no need for a will. If anything is jointly owned (and the joint partner survives), no need for a will.

A will is necessary if other people or children depend on a breadwinner. If both parents die together leaving the children, there should be a will naming a guardian. A will is useful in nominating a personal representative who will handle the "estate," including paying your debts. If there will be people fighting over assets, there should be a will.

Each state has different laws regarding a will. In Colorado, you can handwrite a will so you don't have to use a lawyer. Check your state.

Survivor File

Everyone should have a survivor file. It is a folder, drawer, or box containing documents that specify who should be contacted; list every account and possession, where it is, and what should happen to it; have insurance, Human Resources, Social Security, and Veteran information, as well as funeral arrangements, etc. Inexpensive books like *What My Family Should Know* can be helpful. The survivor file should be updated each year, and of course, family members or friends should know exactly where it is and what it is for.

Legacy Letter

A legacy is what is passed to descendants as well as someone's personal contribution to all mankind in the future. The legacy to your family is your monetary possessions, but more importantly, it includes individual values, accomplishments, and dreams. Everyone should write a legacy letter.

Incapacitated

What is worse than getting hit by a truck and dying? Getting hit by a truck and becoming incapacitated. What is the plan? Who is going to pay the bills? Consider a power of attorney so someone can act in your stead.

Pets

If something happens to a pet owner, the pet will need assistance immediately. Who will do it? Where are the keys to the house? Carry a note about your pet in your wallet. Have a team in place to take control.

Conclusion

Young adults should consult with relatives and friends about their estate planning. It will be easier on you, the beneficiary, when the time comes if it is clear what will happen.

Then put together your own hit-by-a-truck plan, and then use it as a conversation starter with others you care for.

CHAPTER 8

Saving and Investing

Saving 101: She's Twenty and Saves $500 a Month

Best Thing to Do with Your Money

Envelopes and Buckets

Invest My Money: How Do I Do That?

Investing: The Six Nevers

A Savings Mentality: Get It Now!

Think Cash Is Safe? Think Again

What to Know about Financial Advisers

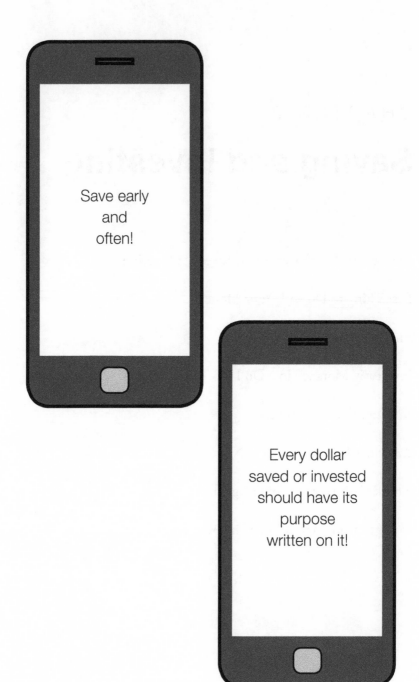

Saving 101: She's Twenty and Saves $500 a Month

Here's how she does that.

I no longer get my haircut at a barbershop. Instead I have a "stylist" named Alicia. When Alicia was twenty, she managed to save $500 each month. As a Money Coach, I want to know how Alicia learned to do that. And what's she saving for? Is there something here that other young people can learn?

At that time, Alicia was an independent contractor at a beauty salon. She determined how much to charge for her services. She paid monthly rent for her chair, and she kept the rest. Alicia has been working since age thirteen, so hard work is nothing new. When Alicia was a teenager, her father, as breadwinner, provided food and shelter; she paid for everything else. Alicia babysat and cleaned houses and went to school. "When you only make a little money, you learn how to make that money last." By the time she turned fourteen, Alicia knew she wanted to work with hair; she acquired a job at a salon at fifteen and started to put money aside for beauty school. She graduated from high school and then from beauty school by age eighteen. Beauty school tuition was paid off by graduation. Alicia bought a car at sixteen (Dad made the payments while she was in beauty school); the five-year loan is almost paid off. Alicia owned a condo (she picked up the payments from what was her mom's condo, and in addition, she made her mom's car payments).

"Stay out of debt" is Alicia's top recommendation for financial success. She got by with one store credit card. When shopping at this store, she put the purchase on her card (to build a credit history), and while still at checkout, she paid off the card with cash. She lives each day following her father's advice: "If you don't have the money, don't buy it." Alicia's suggestion to friends and colleagues is "Sacrifice. Don't give in to the temptations of luxuries while you are young." She would buy her clothes at consignment stores and never pay full price. She packed her lunch and was back at work before her free-spending coworkers returned from the nearby restaurant. Alicia and her boyfriend would go "dutch," and they'd rent movies to watch at home. Alicia knew where every dollar went.

Saving is nothing in itself; saving needs a purpose. Alicia's goal at age twenty was to save $500 each and every month. Some of the saved money went into the "I want to buy a house" bucket. There also was money to build the emergency fund. "I want to save so I'd have six months' worth of expenses in the bank." Alicia learned about rainy days from her father, who was once injured and unable to work for almost a year. The family survived on the emergency fund he had accumulated. Her next goal: learn how to invest for the future.

Money Coach comment: Way to go, Alicia! You are doing everything right with your money. The takeaway—all of us should be like Alicia. Marry someone who shares Alicia's ambitions and initiatives. And, parents, your children learn about money and how to handle it from you. As a parent, you must first have your financial house in order. Then pass on your knowledge to your children.

Best Thing to Do with Your Money: Save It

My dog Zorro (also known as Zorro the Money Dog) does one-minute videos for K–3. Zorro says the best thing you can do with your money is **"Save it for the future."** We all can learn from Zorro, even if we are past the third grade.

An important key to financial success is to **save**. The earlier you start, the more you save, the better your chances of achieving your financial goals. Save early. Save often. Save a little on a regular basis for a long time. Develop a savings mentality early on, and you will be on the right path.

One good rule: **Pay yourself first**. This means savings and investing are the top items on your written monthly budget. (You have a budget, right?) Put money aside first before any other spending, and you will quickly learn that you can live comfortably on what is left. If you plan, as most Americans do, to save what's left at the end of the month, you will find nothing is left. Such is life. If the money is there, you will spend it. Save a percentage of your income each month. When you work, some of this is already done for you. Money is taken from your paycheck for Social Security and Medicare and Unemployment before you receive the paycheck or deposit. You should continue putting money aside for the future by participating in your company's 401(k) or similar retirement plan. Put all you can into savings before you start spending on needs and wants. That save/invest number should be at least 10%. Yes, you can do this!

The reason many cannot save is simple: **we overspend**. I separate spending into three categories:

1. Needs (shelter, food, transportation, clothes, insurance)
2. Wants (just about everything else)
3. Dangerous to your health (smoking, unnecessary amounts of alcohol, drugs, sugary drinks and preprocessed food). Advertising makes us think we need that something being advertised. What happens is that our "needs" become habits, our wants become "needs," and stuff we never intended to buy becomes "I want that." You must take control of what you buy away from the advertising we all see.

Everyone, every month should review money spent on both essentials and non-essentials. If you are not living within your means and/or you cannot pay off your credit cards at the end of the month, you can't afford fast food, Netflix, a car wash, or a tattoo. You must think before you buy, investigate before you buy. Shop with a list, and do not deviate from that list. Too much shopping has become a habit, an expensive habit. Don't buy useless stuff. Change your spending habits. Ask yourself if there is a less expensive alternative. Make your own coffee and lunch. Turn the lights off when you leave the room. Be a kid again. Save up money before buying something. Bring back the piggy bank!

Envelopes and Buckets

As a Money Coach, I encourage using envelopes for the family budget. The use of envelopes is a way to put a cap on spending in selected budget categories.

Envelopes are the adult version of multiple piggy banks. Grandma gives little Johnny $20 for Christmas, and $5 go into the "okay to spend now" piggy bank, $5 into the "save for later" bank, $5 into the "save for college" bank, and $5 into the "help other people" bank. When Johnny asks if he can buy a video game, the answer is "How much have you saved?" To save up money before you buy something is an excellent financial lesson.

The envelope method works best for discretionary spending, things that are not absolutely necessary. If your pet envelope is empty by the tenth of the month and the dog food runs out, you can't let the puppy starve. On the other hand, once your $75 a month envelope for "eating out" is empty, it means you can't eat out anymore that month.

You can either use cash in paper envelopes, or you can use a variety of virtual envelopes (check the app store). You could put the monthly amount for movies on a cash card. You could transfer $500 at the beginning of each month from your checking account where your paycheck is deposited to a savings account and then designate what it is for—for example, $250 to pay down the credit card debt, $100 for the summer vacation, etc. You must, however, keep a running account of the various balances when there are multiple categories in one account. There is even an app for this: Budget Envelopes.

Designating the specific categories is important. You can't have a category such as Sam's Club or Costco or Walmart since you can buy stuff in multiple categories there: gas, tires, furniture, TVs, groceries, pet food. You must be careful with expenses that do not occur monthly, like car insurance. If your car insurance is $600 a year, you must put $50 each month into the envelope so the money is there when the bill arrives.

Another issue is how much to put in each envelope. The answer is to use last year's spending levels to determine this year's spending goals. The key is to track all your expenses so you know where your money goes. The goal is to not spend more than you make.

If you have spending problems, consider using envelopes. Once you've mastered envelopes, go to the next level: buckets. Envelopes are used for line items in your monthly budget; buckets are for larger purchases in the future, things outside your monthly budget.

Buckets of money don't have to be in separate accounts. You can have one online savings account containing several different buckets of money. Start with goals: $400 for a TV; $3,000 for a trip to Romania; $20,000 for that first house. Then find extra money each payday for the bucket account, $1000 with $75 for the TV; $200 for Romania; and the rest for the house. Keep track of the money in each bucket in your "bucket book."

Many people use the pool approach, all their income goes into a checking account, and then they write checks for everything. The problem is that the pool tends to leak. There never seems to be money left over. The pool keeps getting lower and lower. Separate monthly budget items from bucket goals, and start putting money in your buckets.

Young professionals with limited income relative to expenses can use buckets. Buckets are a strong incentive to save. You have a goal; you have saved money for that goal. Now save some more. Buckets help you prioritize where you spend your money.

Managing your money is difficult. I recommend you give the bucket approach a try. It just might work for you. Money is like water; it runs through your hands. Try using buckets.

Invest My Money: How Do I Do That?

Investigate before you invest. It is your money and your responsibility. And your future.

This article covers stocks (equities, ownership in a company) and bonds (lending money to a company or government). Investing involves risk, risk that you can lose some or all your money. Understand the risk. Also, understand the benefit: over the longer term; your investment should outpace inflation. Your invested dollar will buy more in the future.

There are fees when you invest. Understand the fees, and select investments with low fees.

There are two main ways to invest: automatically and when you decide. You can set up automatic deductions from your paycheck to go into your 401(k) or similar retirement plan. Working with your bank, you can set up periodic purchases into an IRA or into a regular investment account. Check the fees; a $5 transaction fee has minimal impact on a $2,000 investment, a large impact on a $100 investment. You yourself can make the investments on your own schedule. If you do the investment yourself online, there often will be a small transaction fee. Any fee under $10 is acceptable. If you call and have a person make the investment, there could be a much larger fee—$40 and above. Mutual funds and ETFs (exchange-traded fund) also have annual fees, which are "hidden fees," fees that are not noticeable by looking at statements, but the fees are listed on the investment information page. Check these fees before you buy. The best way to invest is automatically. Pay yourself (invest) first before you pay the bills.

I do not recommend buying individual stocks; invest in a multitude of stocks through an index mutual fund (been around a long time) or the newer less-expensive ETF. You buy a mutual fund directly from a mutual fund company, like Vanguard or Fidelity or T. Rowe Price. Generally, there are no transaction fees when you buy mutual funds directly from the company. Mutual funds are traded daily, but the purchase or sale price is determined after the stock market closes once all the underlying stock and/or bond values for the day are totaled. ETFs trade like stocks—all day when the stock market is opened. ETFs are purchased through your brokerage account; there often is a transaction fee. Deal only with "discount" brokers, such as Vanguard or TDAmeritrade, where the fees are much less. And beginning August 2018, Vanguard is dropping transaction fees on many ETFs. If you are comfortable going online and opening an account, do so because your range of financial companies is large. If you must talk to someone and you live in Colorado Springs, visit the TDAmeritrade office in the Antlers hotel downtown (on February 23, 2018, Scottrade became part of TDAmeritrade). Sorry, the local T. Rowe Price office no longer takes walk-ins. The trend is online. Of course, when your company sponsors a 401(k) or similar retirement plan, you must deal with the plan administrator which has its own list of funds.

How many different mutual funds or ETFs should you hold in your investment account? Keep it simple. There are thousands of choices; all you really need is one, two, three—max four. I personally have a mutual fund account at T. Rowe Price and brokerage accounts at Vanguard, E*Trade, and TDAmeritrade. Vanguard, which is customer owned and the longtime low-cost leader, also has regular mutual fund accounts.

When it comes to investments, there are two major types: index funds, which hold all the stocks in whatever index it follows, and managed funds, where the managers select the underlying stocks and/or bonds that they think will do best. Index funds, which are cheaper, are clear winners. Compared to managed funds, index funds win about 85% of the time.

If you want one and only one investment, I suggest the T. Rowe Price global allocation fund, which has stocks (60%), bonds (30%), alternatives (10%). The annual fee is 0.84%, which is higher than most; 75% of the ETF industry's recent inflows have gone to funds with an annual expense ratio of 0.20% or less. There are 123 ETFs with expenses of 0.10% or less (2018). Another single investment would be a target date fund, where the holdings automatically become more conservative (fewer stocks, more bonds) as you move toward your retirement date.

ETFs have two to four letters; mutual funds have five letters.

If you want just two ETF holdings, you can check the following:
- [ ] VT – Vanguard Total World, US and foreign stocks
- [ ] BND – Vanguard Total Bond Market, US bonds

If you want just three mutual fund holdings, you can check the following:
- [ ] VTSMX – Vanguard Total Stock Index
- [ ] VGTSX – Vanguard Total International Stock Index
- [ ] VBMFX – Vanguard Total Bond Index (or RPSIX, T. Rowe Price New Income)

This is just a start; there are many more combinations. The more you have, the harder to understand and manage.

You must balance your holdings between stocks and bonds. I recommend for most no more than 50% stocks nor less than 20% stocks. I favor an equal balance between US and foreign stocks.

Once your portfolio is established, you must rebalance annually. That means if you have a 50%–50% balance between stocks and bonds, and after a year, it is 60% stocks, then you sell stocks and buy bonds to bring it back to 50/50. And once you have your portfolio, remember, it is for the long term. Don't check it each day with worry in mind.

Remember the **golden rules of investing**, never to be forgotten: Do not buy a financial product recommended by someone who makes a commission on the transaction. Take investment advice only from a fiduciary, someone legally bound to put you, the client, first. Ask your adviser if he/she is a fiduciary.

Your home is a good investment, although technically it is not part of your portfolio. Property, be it your home or rental or business property, is a good long-term investment. Buy a house!

When should you start investing? Now!

Investing: The Six Nevers

Never invest in
1. anything you don't understand,
2. anything that has a sales charge, either up front or when you sell,
3. anything that has a "surrender fee,"
4. something where you must "sign here and now" (use the twenty-four-hour rule; tell salespeople you need twenty-four hours to think about it),
5. anything that sounds too good to be true,
6. anything recommended by someone who makes a commission on the product.

Know that financial salesmen and saleswomen will try to convince you that investing is too complicated for you. They want you to turn your money over to them so they can collect fee after fee after fee. Your money goes into their pockets.

Always use common sense.

Investing is not that complicated. Learn how to do it yourself. Begin today!

A Savings Mentality: Get It Now!

It is never too late to start saving. But first you need to develop a savings mentality. The earlier you start, the better your life will be.

Saving money is an acquired skill. Many of us learn from our parents, but too many adults do not have a clue, and their kids suffer.

Our culture is partly to blame:

☐ We tend to live for the moment, not for the future.
☐ We consume rather than save. We replace rather than fix.
☐ We waste. American families throw away more than $2,000 in food each year, just from the freezer.

Our priorities are wrong. I have lived in Africa, where most are poor. The very top priority in an African family is money to buy school uniforms and supplies for their children. Attending school is generally free, but you must have a uniform and supplies.

We think we know it all. The US is not in the top ten in these categories:

☐ Safest countries
☐ Highest quality of life
☐ Best for children
☐ Best healthcare

"Change" is the key word when it comes to saving money. Step back and evaluate how and where you spend your money, and then change the way you do things. Change comes hard, but it is absolutely necessary. Self-assessment is essential. Also, learn from those around you; work with friends and family, and educate yourself. Friends can become savings buddies, with whom you can share ideas on practical ways to save for the future. Put together a support group.

Not everything is fixed price. Check ads on your phone. Compare prices; bargain. A client recently saved $750 on a mattress by taking a strong bargaining position.

Saving must be the top item on your budget. Do it first. Earmark every saved dollar with its purpose. Don't save to just "save." Have goals.

Once you start moving forward on saving money, it becomes a habit. This is one habit you want to keep for the rest of your life.

Begin to save now! Get that **savings mentality**!

Think Cash Is Safe? Think Again

As a Money Coach, it is a big challenge when I talk to people who have all their savings and investments in cash. "I don't want to risk losing any of my money" is the typical argument. The real risk, I counter, is losing purchasing power. The risk is called inflation, which is "a general increase in prices and fall in the purchasing value of money."

There are many statistics for inflation, but what it comes down to is how much you and your family pay for the specific things you buy. For me, gasoline cost about $0.25 a gallon when I started to drive many years ago. What if I had put $1.00, four gallons' worth, under my mattress and take it to the gas station today? If you are early in your work life and plan to live many more years, inflation matters.

Everyone needs a balanced savings and investment portfolio. That means stocks and bonds, I-Bonds, real estate, and other investments in addition to cash. The reality is, your dollar will not buy as much in the future. If you are currently losing 2% to inflation on $100,000 because you are earning little or no interest, that's $2,000 a year or $5.50 each day. Then consider a more normal inflation rate of 4% and think about twenty, forty, sixty years. If you were born in 1985 and your parents purchased something for $10, in 2018, that $10 item would cost $23.43.

Cash is a huge risk:

- ☐ Savings account interest rate: 2010 0.19%   2018 0.05%
- ☐ Checking account interest rate: 2010 0.11%   2018 0.04%
- ☐ Dow Jones Stock Market Index: 2010 10,400   2018 26,062

Yes, have some money in cash to pay the monthly bills. Yes, have money in cash for emergencies. Use an online bank like Ally. com. Connect your checking account to the online account and transfer money electronically back and forth. Ally rate in February 2019 is 2.2%. Consider I-Bonds for part of your emergency fund (you cannot withdraw without penalty for five years).

Do not have money in the stock market you will need in the next five years. Move into the stock market slowly. The best strategy is to invest the same amount each month or each quarter. That way, when the stock market is low, you buy more shares, and when the market is high, you buy fewer shares. Works out to your advantage in the long run.

An important key to successful money management is diversification. Keep your money in a variety of places.

What to Know about Financial Advisers

Many people turn over management of their investment portfolios to financial professionals. This could be a mistake. You are the CEO (chief executive officer, the one who makes the final decisions) of your money. Financial professionals are just advisers. It is your money; you must take control!

Among financial services professionals surveyed, 24% believe they "may need to engage in unethical or illegal conduct in order to be successful" (survey by New York law firm Labaton Sucharow; reported in *Investment Advisor* magazine, August 2012). That's not one bad apple in a barrel; that's one bad apple out of four.

How can you tell if your money is with that bad apple? Here are three red flags:

Red flag 1: The financial professional who manages your money is not a fiduciary. The "general purpose of an adviser's fiduciary duty is to eliminate conflicts of interest and prevent an adviser from taking advantage of a client's trust" ("Fiduciary Duty: Best Practices for Fulfilling Suitability Obligations," *Investment Advisor* magazine, June 2012). As a registered investment adviser, I have that fiduciary responsibility, and I take it very seriously. A broker and many who call themselves financial representatives do not. Many in the industry are fighting to keep from becoming a fiduciary. Some say the fiduciary status does not fit their business model. Can you imagine a business model where the customer is not placed first?

Red flag 2: The financial adviser makes a commission on a financial produce he or she recommends. From experience, there are too many opportunities for conflict of interest when you are sold a product that benefits the salesperson.

Red flag 3: You can't get a straight answer when you ask, "What is the total dollar amount of fees on my investment portfolio?" There are a number of fees on investments—some difficult to find, some totally hidden. Fees on a self-directed portfolio of exchange-traded funds (ETFs) should be in the neighborhood of .25% or less of the total portfolio value. Fidelity now has several ETFs at 0%. A broker may say his fee is 1%. That is "his" fee; he doesn't mention the annual fee on the underlying funds, which can be another 1% or the 3% fees some annuities carry.

Make sure you are not dealing with a bad apple. Investigate before you invest.

And shame on those bad apples.

CHAPTER 9

Protecting Your Money

Protect Your Assets

Avoid Pressure from Financial Salespeople

Do I Need Life Insurance?

Beware of financial salespeople!

On railroad tracks, stop, look, listen. With your money: the same!

Protect Your Assets

You have money and other possessions. Now you must guard against losing these assets. There are predators and scammers who want your money and your stuff. And there are unexpected events that can cause you to lose your possessions. Here are some guidelines:

- ☐ **Avoid financial salespersons.** Avoid people trying to sell you a financial product on which they make a commission. You must be in overall charge of your assets.

- ☐ **Protect your data.** Have copies of credit cards and driver license and all other cards in your wallet. Keep your passport locked in a safe. Start a survivor file. Don't respond to emails, texts, or phone calls that don't look right. Protect your digital assets and change passwords often.

- ☐ **Have plenty of insurance.** This includes health insurance, dental insurance, disability insurance, home or renter insurance, automobile insurance, life insurance (if someone else depends on you), umbrella insurance (to up your liability coverage). Let neighbors know when you are away. Write down information on your pet, what to do if something happens to you.

- ☐ **Avoid some insurance.** Because some insurance is sold by fear, beware and investigate mortgage life insurance (rely on term), credit card losses (usually limited), car rental (your credit card or own auto insurance often covers this), flight life insurance (term), cancer insurance (rely on health insurance), involuntary unemployment insurance (emergency fund and unemployment), accidental death insurance (stick with term).

- ☐ **Save for a rainy day.** You **must** build a substantial emergency fund. Stuff happens that is not in the budget yet must be paid for. If you borrow for emergencies, your financial life will get worse.

- ☐ **Consider Mother Nature.** This includes contingencies for electricity outages (how will you recharge your cell phone or cook dinner), fire mitigation, earthquakes, road closures.

Plan for disasters like water contamination or cutoff (have extra supply of drinking water). Have candles or flashlights or fully charged cell phones to see in the dark.

☐ **Avoid dangerous activities.** Inattentive driving (driving while talking, texting, drinking, not watching the road), walking alone, doing drugs, and smoking.

☐ **Do health planning.** Know where the nearest hospital or urgent care facility is; have medication and allergy information on your person and on your refrigerator. Keep fit, exercise, and eat right.

☐ **Make a hit-by-a-truck plan.** Know what is covered by beneficiary or payable-upon-death designations. Write a will if you need one. Determine who will pay your bills if you cannot, who will make financial decisions if you are not able, what happens to the kids if both parents pass. Write your legacy letter. Your legacy is what you pass on to your descendants as well as your personal contribution to all mankind in the future. Your legacy to your family is your monetary possessions, but more importantly, it is your values, your accomplishments, your dreams.

☐ **Avoid pyramid schemes.** These schemes are promoted as a business opportunity with little effort on your part—chain letters, junk email, buying clubs. You pay an upfront fee, and then all you do is recruit others who in turn will recruit others, hence the name pyramid. You get "profits" from the "sales" of those under you. It's similar to legitimate multilevel marketing plans, but there generally is little to sell. The whole thing revolves around recruiting additional people. Avoid any plan that offers commissions to recruit new distributors. Beware of plans that ask you to buy costly inventory. Don't sign contracts when under high-pressure tactics.

☐ **Use common sense.** Life insurance is insurance, not an investment. Buy term life insurance if someone else depends on your income. Look out for get-rich schemes. If it looks too good to be true, it probably is a scam. Don't ask a tire dealer if you need new tires. Insert a quarter into the tire's tread with Washington's head toward the tire. If no portion of his head is covered, you need new tires (AARP). Don't ask a mutual fund salesperson if you need a mutual fund. Avoid the commission and high fees. Go to a low-fee company, such as Vanguard, and buy direct.

☐ **Be prepared.** Follow the Boy Scout motto.
☐ **Be an informed voter.** Know well that big companies/ organizations pay "bribes" through lobbyists to reap money benefits to them, not you. Know your candidate; seek campaign reform.

Just be careful!

Avoid Pressure from Financial Salespeople

Many financial people are just salesmen or saleswomen. They are more interested in commissions than in helping your finances. One of their favorite tactics is to scare people into buying their products.

An ad starts out with "I lost half my investment assets in both 2001 and 2008" and goes on to promote buying houses instead. The targets are those people who are worried about volatility in the stock market. Remember, you should always own some stocks.

Another one may say, "Don't run out of money—buy my annuity." An annuity is like Social Security. You put money in, and when you retire, you get a monthly check. But most people who buy annuities never start taking the money out. Ask yourself, whom do you want to totally control your money—you or an insurance company?

A reverse mortgage is a way to take money from the equity in your home. But the Consumer Financial Protection Bureau found the advertising contains "confusing, incomplete, and inaccurate statements" and that most people do not have a clue on how the loan works. Reverse mortgages are a last resort.

Here are some rules to protect yourself and your money:

- ☐ Rule 1: Realize that it is your money and your money is your responsibility. You can ask for help, but you must maintain responsibility over your money.
- ☐ Rule 2: Only buy financial or insurance products that have no sales fees.
- ☐ Rule 3: Be careful of inviting a salesperson into your house. He or she won't leave until you buy something. Tell him/her about the twenty-four-hour rule. You never buy anything without thinking about it for twenty-four hours.
- ☐ Rule 4: Make sure you fully understand how the product you are buying works. If it comes with a twenty-five-page explanation, don't buy it.
- ☐ Rule 5: Seek advice only from someone you can trust. Ask the person you are talking to if he/she is a fiduciary, someone bound by law to put your interests over their own.

Also, be aware of the biggest myth in the financial industry: "Investments are too complicated for you to understand. I will show you the way." In reality, investing is not that hard.

Here's the guidance:

- ☐ Save as much as you can.
- ☐ Learn the basics of investing.
- ☐ Spread your money between stocks, bonds, cash, and other investments.
- ☐ Use low-cost financial companies. Call Vanguard. They will help you establish a mutual fund or a brokerage account online. If you want to sit down with a live person, check which discount firms have a local office.
- ☐ Stay away from financial salespeople! It's your money, not theirs.

Do I Need Life Insurance?

"Do I need life insurance?" This is a very important question when thinking about family finances. But you should be very careful to whom you ask this question. If you ask a life insurance salesperson, know well that the answer will be yes. This is because his/her job is to sell life insurance. Since life insurance can have one of the highest commissions in the financial industry, you must get your recommendation from someone who is not focused on a commission.

In most cases, you need life insurance only when someone else depends upon you for income. This means children don't need life insurance. The death of a child is one of life's greatest tragedies, but it is not an economic tragedy. If you are married and have children or if you depend upon your spouse to pay the bills, the key years to be covered by life insurance are after you marry or after you have children to when the kids leave home and are on their own financially. Remember that the insurance may be needed to fund higher education for family members. And it is not just the breadwinner who should be covered. If a stay-at-home mom dies, there will be a financial shock also.

There are two main types of life insurance: whole life and term. With whole life, commonly called cash value, you pay extra in premiums and your policy has a cash value that you can take out if you no longer need life insurance. With term, you are covered for a certain amount of time, and then the coverage expires. You can obtain multiple policies covering different periods of your life at different coverage levels.

Which type? Most crucial question is how much insurance is needed rather than what type. If a large amount is needed, term may be the answer because you can get more coverage with less money. The only logical reason to purchase cash value insurance is that it is superior to the other investment alternatives. I think life insurance should have only one goal—to insure a life. Invest the difference in premiums elsewhere.

How much insurance? Generally, more than you think. You need to determine how much annual income will be needed and for how long.

Bottom line: make sure you have adequate life insurance for your personal situation.

CHAPTER 10

Married with Money (and Kids)

Married with Money before "I Do"

Married with Debt

Your Children and Money

Your Task as a New Parent

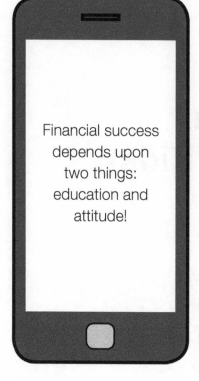

Financial success depends upon two things: education and attitude!

As parents, what will you teach your kids about money?

Married with Money before "I Do"

Money can be a major irritant in a marriage. Stay focused on your commitment to each other and the values you admire in your partner. Marriage and money are both two-way streets. You must establish goals together. You must work together to reach those goals.

The Money Talk

The to-be-married couple should sit down shortly after the engagement and ask each other questions about their respective money lives. Start with elementary school and continue to the present. How do you view spending, debt, saving? What are your financial goals? Then I suggest you talk about money on a regular basis. Talk about issues as they come up, but don't get bogged down in disagreements. Most important is to schedule a time to talk only about money issues. Limit the time to thirty or forty-five minutes, and plan to hold sessions once or twice a month. After the talk, reward yourself by going out to dinner.

No Surprises

There should be no money surprises after the wedding. Full disclosure before the wedding is absolutely necessary. Devote one sit-down-and-discuss session to this important issue. Don't be judgmental, but share your ideals and goals and understand your partner's ideals and goals. Debt, bankruptcies, spending habits, and attitude toward spending and savings are all important and necessary topics.

Combining the Finances

Join the money from two individuals together to form one family unit. How to do that? Pool the resources or keep them separate? Keep in mind that there is no right or wrong answer. It depends on the two of you. Separate accounts are a key to maintaining identity and a necessary sense of independence. Separate accounts allow for the spontaneity of individual consumption. This may mean money spent on a night out or tickets to a Broncos game. For others, it may mean extra clothes or shoes. It is extremely important, even priceless, to have one's spouse "feel good." Have a separate budget category for each spouse like "feel-good things," but I caution you not to use the word "allowance" when figuring this out. I recommend three accounts: his account, her account, and a family account. This gives each a separate source of money and yet pays the bills. How do you put money into these three accounts? Many different ways. If both of you are working, come up with a prorated basis. Many working couples bank one paycheck and use the other.

Problem comes when one works and one stays home to raise the kids. Who's going to be in charge of the finances and make investment decisions? Who pays the bills? Who decides what to buy and how much to pay? The answer is both of you. There should be something for each spouse to do, but most of the decisions should be made together. Talk about it, be flexible, and then talk about it some more.

Bottom Line

It is important to realize that you don't have to come up with a "solution" to an issue quickly. Decisions can be implemented gradually as the marriage grows and as you become more comfortable with each other and each other's money life. The goal is to create an environment in which finances within the marriage will work. It matters less how you end up doing something than the fact you work together. The bottom line is simple. You are starting a life together, and you must try and try and try to be on the same page **together**.

Married with Debt

They say that love is blind, but that is not a good thing when it comes to the financial side of marriage. Long before the wedding day, the couple must have the money talk. Everything financial must be on the table for discussion—no money secrets before a marriage.

Red flags to watch out for during the talk:

- ☐ Bankruptcy in the past with no plans to pay the money back. Fact is, when you borrow money, you must pay it back. Bankruptcy removes the legal reason to do so, but it does not take away the moral obligation to repay your debts. Remember that "I do" also is a moral obligation.
- ☐ Combined credit score of less than 1400. Credit problems have the potential to sink a marriage right from the start.
- ☐ Combined total of more than four credit cards. Most people are fine with one to two credit cards. Any more indicates a possible problem, especially if any are maxed out. And of course, a credit card should not be used by anyone who cannot pay the full balance at the end of each month.
- ☐ Combined emergency fund of less than $4,000. An emergency fund is absolutely necessary for everybody and especially for a newlywed couple. A wedding gift to an emergency fund is better than a toaster any day.

If the money talk uncovers a problem, that problem must be acknowledged, and a plan must be written to solve that problem.

Each party should have eyes wide open when it comes to the spending habits of the potential partner. We are looking for responsible behavior here.

When you get married, you want to acquire a loving and responsible mate. You do not want to acquire a pile of debt and lack of financial common sense.

Your Children and Money

As parents, one of our most important responsibilities is to teach our children about money. It is also one of the most difficult. My advice is to start early, never let up, as well as to guide, direct, suggest, coach, supervise. And most importantly, be a good example!

When do you teach children about money? Nonstop. The goal is for them to understand that money represents hard work. Tell them you have learned a secret on how to make money—going to work. Money must be treated with loving care and should never, ever be wasted.

Explain to your children that money can be cash or it can be a check, a debit card, or electronic money. It is important for them to understand that noncash "money" is still money. Many of us enter the world of debt through the overuse of credit cards because using the card somehow seems "different" than spending dollar bills. Money is money! It must be spent very carefully.

One of the best ways to teach your children about money is to provide them with their own income, an allowance. I agree with the many childcare specialists who recommend allowances be paid unrelated to required chores and other responsibilities like homework. Chores and homework can be linked to other incentives or to privileges withheld. Pay the allowance no matter what. Pay it on a regular basis—the same day, the same time, and the same place. Never forget and always have the correct amount available. The amount depends on your income and the child's age. It doesn't have to be a lot, but it must be something your child can see and touch and something he or she expects on a regular basis. Paying an allowance does not necessarily mean coming up with "extra" money from an already tight budget. Simply take some of the money you already spend on the child for candy or clothes or toys and give it to your youngster and say, "Here is your allowance. This is your money."

Once you decide on the amount for the allowance, work with your child to develop a savings and spending plan. Ask your child to be accountable for money spent, but avoid questioning purchase decisions. Stress that the allowance must last for the entire period and that once it is spent, it is gone and will not be replaced. The child must wait until the next allowance payment. Most of us understand the trade-off between spending now and saving for later. Pay your child for doing extra chores or saving the family money like turning off the lights to save electricity. Share your child's excitement as the pile of money grows. When enough is saved, make it a special family event to go to the store and buy the item. Congratulate your youngster on his or her ability to save for a special purchase. A lesson learned here will last a lifetime.

Let your children see where the household money goes. Let them watch you write checks to pay the bills. Explain what each check is for and how it benefits all family members. Set aside cash for groceries, and let them help you make price comparisons at the store. If the item is for them, let them actually pay the money to the clerk at the store. Show them how to count the change, and teach them that anytime anyone gives them money, they must count it to make sure it is the right amount. Discuss matters involving money with the kids on a regular basis, perhaps at family meetings.

Use the media as a tool to educate the children about financial matters. You will find that as children get older, they listen more to their peers and to the environment outside the home than they do to Mom and Dad (anyway, that's how it happened in our home). Newspapers and the internet and TV often have more credibility than parents. Encourage thought-provoking reading, listening, and surfing.

Don't forget to talk about taxes. Prepare your young adult for paycheck shock—the fact that once they get a job, the paycheck is less than the number of hours worked times the hourly pay rate. Few teens understand that the employer pays Social Security taxes over and above the amount deducted from the paycheck. Explain at an early age that taxes are a key component of government. Every working person and every employer must pay taxes for services ranging from national defense to road repair. Taxes can influence purchasing decisions. For example, taxes on liquor and tobacco are high in order to discourage use. There also are tax incentives to buy a house or to give to a charity. Explain what sales tax is and why it changes from one city to the next or why there is no sales tax on a military base.

As you already know, each child is different. When dealing with money and children, you will find you must try many things before you find something that works. But the key is to keep trying. Me? I've tried just about everything with my three kids, who are now all in their thirties and forties. I tried extra money for good grades (generally didn't work but was worth the try), a bimonthly clothing allowance (worked very well with one), a down payment for a car if no school was missed as a senior (she got the car). The point is to find out what works with each child and have him or her buy into the concept.

A note of caution: "Loan" to me, a dad, means the money will be paid back. "Loan" to an offspring of any age means "gift." Get it in writing.

Age Guidance

Remember that each child is different.
- Ages 0–6: Open a 529 college savings plan. Encourage family donations.
- Ages 1–6: Frame a stock certificate from a company the child will recognize (Disney or McDonald's) on the child's bedroom wall. Prompt discussion about owning part of a large company through investing.
- Ages 4–6: Begin allowance or payment for small jobs around the house. Emphasize wise spending and saving.
- Ages 5–8: Separate the child's allowance (income) into short- and long-term spending and savings and into charitable giving categories.
- Ages 6–12: Start simple investment decisions in companies the child recognizes. Increase allowance, but make the child start paying for things he wants (not needs).
- Ages 10–14: Discuss the rise and fall of stocks, bonds, and mutual funds. Begin risk/return talks. Find a company a child likes, and follow it with him/her.
- Ages 12–14: Talk about what it takes to be independent and living on own.

□ Ages 13–16: Increase allowance to pay and budget for almost all purposes.
□ Ages 12–17: Open a custodial Roth IRA account, and match any income the child contributes. Agree that no money is to be withdrawn before retirement.
□ Ages 16–17: Open a checking account with the child's money.

And finally, good luck!

Your Task as a New Parent

As new parents, it is your duty to teach money sense to your children.

Kids learn from observing how Mom and Dad do things.

Always explain to little Billy that the money you take from an ATM is money that Mommy and Daddy have earned by working and put into the bank for safekeeping. We don't want our kids to think money grows inside ATMs.

If we want our kids to save for the future, they must observe us saving for the future. A good way to teach the kids about saving is to open a 529 college savings plan for each child. When they reach kindergarten, start explaining the plan and eventually help them contribute to their own future education.

I had a client couple who used to yell at each other in front of their young son when paying the bills. Just think how this young man will approach bill paying when he grows up.

Kids will pick up on our irresponsible behavior very quickly. Be responsible!

I learned many things about money from my mom and dad.

Mom and Money

On the rare occasion when we ate out, Mom would take leftover food home for another meal.

Mom would make clothes for us kids. We would only get new clothes when something wore out completely.

Mom had a cookie jar where she put money left over from the grocery shopping.

Mom would can fruit and vegetables in the fall for use during the winter.

Mom was always looking for bargains. I used to think she would buy ten garbage cans if she could get them for the price of five. She would often tell the store clerk, "I saw this on sale last week, and I would like that sale price now."

I have lived in Africa for four years, where I learned to bargain for everything. Mom would be proud of me for this.

Mom taught me to always check my change to make sure it was right.

Dad and Money

Dad would tell me not to use a credit card, that I should use cash instead.

Dad said I could drive the car only if I paid for the insurance. So I got a job.

Dad always insisted I not buy anything unless I had saved the money first.

Assignment for All Those in Their Twenties and Thirties

Think about your childhood and money.

Write down three positive things you learned from your parents about money.

Write down three things you wished your parents had taught you about money.

Discuss with your spouse how these lessons are learned, and the wish list can be used to instruct your own young children. Kids begin to understand money concepts as early as age three. Make it a point to talk about money whenever you buy something. Little Billy must understand that he can't have everything.

Remember

Parents are key to responsible children when it comes to money. The kids watch everything you do. Do it right!

CHAPTER 11

Taxes

Taxes: What You Really Need to Know

What Should I Do with My Income Tax Refund?

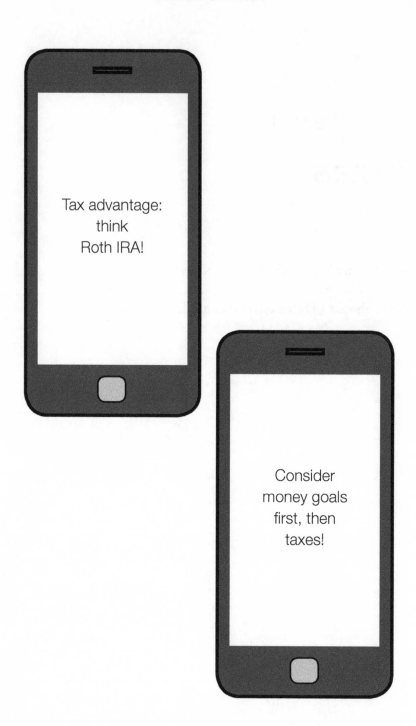

Taxes: What You Really Need to Know

Most people look at taxes the wrong way. We hate to pay taxes, hate to prepare taxes, and even hate to think about taxes. Wrong attitude! What you don't know about your taxes will adversely affect your finances.

Taxes are necessary for every public service we enjoy. You want schools, roads, police, and military? You pay taxes. We pay sales tax (same rate for everyone) to state and local governments. We pay income tax (progressive rate—the more you earn, the higher the rate) at the federal and state levels. We pay property tax (school, library, etc.). We pay "use" tax (toll roads). Food items are generally not taxed. Other things we buy daily are usually taxed at the sales tax rate.

Your employer pays these over and above your salary:

☐ Unemployment taxes
☐ Federal Insurance Contributions Act (FICA), Social Security, and Medicare taxes

For 2019, the Social Security tax rate is 6.2% on the first $132,900 wages paid. The Medicare tax rate is 1.45% on the first $200,000 and 2.35% above $200,000.

You have tax deductions taken out of every paycheck. You pay an identical amount of FICA taxes, Social Security 6.2%, and Medicare 1.45%. Then you have a designated amount of withholding to pay your annual income tax (so you are not hit with a large amount at tax time).

Unfortunately, most Americans don't understand the basics of our tax system. Everyone should know his/her marginal tax bracket and, more importantly, what marginal tax bracket means. We pay taxes at several different rates. Per the 2017 tax law, some income for 2018 and beyond is taxed at 0%, some is taxed at 10%, and the rates go up from there depending on your income: 22%, 24%, 32%, 35%, 37%. The marginal rate is the highest rate we pay. Understand that if our marginal rate is 24%, we don't pay 24% on all our income. We pay 24% on the last dollar we earn and 24% on each additional dollar until we reach the next highest tax bracket. But wait, it is not as easy as that. Some income, such as qualified dividends and capital gains, is taxed at 0% or 15% or 20%, depending on which tax bracket you are in. Add your income from all sources. Subtract "adjustments." Then subtract "deductions," either standard or itemized. You pay zero tax on adjustments and deductions. Now subtract the total of your qualified dividends and capital gains, on which you pay 0%, 15%, or 20%. What remains is taxed at the various rates, 10%, 22%, etc.

A good goal, in my opinion, is to be taxed at the highest rate, because that means you are making much more money than the rest of it. Being married and having an adjusted gross income of $612,350 or more equals the 37% tax bracket. For each dollar over that, the government takes $0.37, and you keep $0.63. Do not avoid making more money because you don't want to pay taxes on additional earned income.

Penalties

Our culture and training tells us to "defer" taxes. That's how IRA and 401(k) money works. That's what happens when we bring deductions into the current tax year and push income into the next. When we defer taxes, there are consequences that should be considered penalties:

Penalty 1: We must pay taxes somewhere down the line. "Defer" means to put off, not eliminate.

Penalty 2: We may move some income into higher tax categories when we defer taxes. You put money into an employer 401(k), so you must pay your taxes on your contributions when the money comes out. And the money must come out starting at age seventy and a half; it is called required minimum distribution (RMD). For many people, the extra money from RMD pushes them into higher tax brackets. The result is that you have a higher tax rate as a senior than you would have if you had paid taxes when you received the dollars years ago. (This is a good argument for a Roth account, see below.) The growth of your contributions through dividends and capital gains, however, is not taxed at the lower "capital gains" rate in retirement accounts when it is taken out of a retirement plan but at the higher "income rate." You are paying more taxes than you would if you had just invested the money in a regular account and paid only on the capital gains. This penalty applies to annuities also; often the annuity salesman doesn't explain this tax fact.

Penalty 3: My view is that taxes are relatively low now. Taxes will be higher in the future (some of the so-called tax breaks in the 2017 law will expire in 2025). If I'm correct, we will be deferring taxes so we can pay more tax in the future.

Tax Action Plan

If you want to use taxes to your advantage, make the following three-steps to your tax action plan:

1. Do your own taxes. You will better understand the tax system. And save money.
2. Change your attitude on taxes. Say, "I want to pay taxes now, not in the future."
3. Put your money into a Roth IRA or Roth 401k (if available) instead of a regular IRA or regular 401(k) so it will never be taxed again. Roth IRA contributions are taxed the year you put them into the account, but that money and the decades of growth are never taxed again, a real tax bonus.

Make it a goal to understand the tax system and keep up to date on changes.

What Should I Do with My Income Tax Refund?

We all need to carefully plan how we use our tax refund money. These dollars should be a big part of your financial planning. Never take out a loan to get your refund early.

If you receive a big refund, you are not in control of your finances. You can reduce taxes withheld so you will have a smaller tax refund next year. But be careful; the extra cash each pay period must be used intelligently.

If you don't have an emergency fund, use the tax refund money to start or build your current emergency fund. An emergency fund is a top priority for everyone. Without it, you eventually will suffer a financial disaster.

If you owe credit card or other debt, then, yes, use the money to pay down that debt but only after you have solved the problem that led to the debt. The problem probably is overspending. Work on your budget. Tighten your spending.

Debt is often related to not having an emergency fund, so if you have these two problems together, I would split the refund check between the two.

Saving and investing are good options for this unexpected cash. If your financial situation will be the same this year as last, divide the refund amount by 52 (if paid weekly) or 26 (if paid every two weeks), and ask your employer to add that amount to your 401(k) each pay period. Or have the money deposited directly into a separate savings account.

The worst thing you can do with your refund is to put it in your checking account without a designated purpose. I can just about guarantee it will disappear within three to four months. The idea is to use the money to advance your financial situation, not fritter it away.

Planning what to do with your tax refund is serious business. Put together a written plan and follow that plan to the letter. Then adjust your finances so next year you will not have a big refund or use the refund as outlined above.

CHAPTER 12
Travel

Why Travel Abroad?

Learn to Travel on the Cheap

Travel Tips

Planning Self-Travel: The Top 5

Why Travel Abroad?

Most of my focus as a Money Coach is on saving money. But if you have more money coming in than going out, you have a substantial emergency fund, and you're paying off your credit cards each month, it is time to find something you are passionate about and just do it. My suggestion is travel—specifically, foreign travel. It will increase your knowledge and give you a better appreciation of the world we live in.

Fear of foreigners and racial and religious bigotry, unfortunately, have come center stage in the United States. We must remember we all came from somewhere else. If you go back far enough, that includes Native Americans. When we experience other cultures, it gives us a new perspective on people in our world. It is a most valuable contribution to our education.

When I say travel abroad, I mean get off the beaten path and see how others live. Staying at Club Med and four or five-star hotels where they serve hamburgers and everyone speaks English is not foreign travel. I have traveled widely and have lived in Africa, Asia, and the Caribbean. I have seen hardworking people who waste nothing; I've seen happy kids playing in the most remote places. I have come to appreciate other cultures and realize that "foreigners" often do things better than we do.

Here are a couple of examples:

☐ I asked a young lady in Hong Kong why the Chinese read their books "backward" (i.e., back to front). She said most Chinese are right handed, and then she demonstrated that turning pages the Chinese way is a more natural motion than the way we do it. Think about it.

☐ In Uganda, the girls were getting their hair done, and this takes a long, long time. So I was talking to the local kids and passing out stuff I had picked up on the airplane. I gave a nine-year-old a small packet of pepper. I told him it was pepper and *pilipili* in Swahili. He still did not understand what it was. The question Americans would ask in this situation is "What is it?" The question the nine-year-old asked me was "How is it used?" which, of course, is the exact right way to find out.

Speaking of Uganda, I talked to a couple from Uganda who were touring the US to promote their nonprofit, which helps pregnant teens. They relate that many Americans ask where Uganda is and often say they believe Africa is a single country (there are fifty-four countries in Africa). The solution to ignorance is education, and one good way to educate yourself about other cultures is to travel abroad.

Travel if you can. You don't have to go that far or spend a lot of money to learn about other cultures. The Hopi Reservation in Arizona has a vastly different culture. Befriend people in your hometown who come from another culture. It will be an educational experience.

Let's get on the road again and educate ourselves and our children. Traveling is an excellent way to spend your hard-earned money. And you will be the better for it.

Learn to Travel on the Cheap

One of the best investments is education. Education takes place in the classroom, but real learning happens through experience. There is no better place to learn about our nation and our world than to travel. Years ago, I had an idea for travel in the United States: make sure you keep in touch with friends and relatives living every four hundred to five hundred miles in all directions from your home across the entire country. Take a road trip. Arrive late in the afternoon, have dinner, stay the night, have breakfast, pack a lunch, and leave midmorning for your next destination. Repeat. Repeat. Try it. It works as long as you don't wear out your welcome.

Some of the best travel is to foreign countries, especially places where the culture is different from what we experience day to day. Our culture is our culture, but it is not the only culture, and it is best if we learn this early. If you can visit someone you know abroad, the experience can be priceless as well as relatively inexpensive. When traveling abroad, don't go first class and stay at four or five-star hotels, where everyone speaks English; stay with the locals if possible or a small hotel. Don't eat at McDonald's; eat off the beaten path. Don't be a "tourist." Consider yourself to be on an educational adventure. Get off the tourist bus. Learn how to use local transportation. Use a guidebook. I like the *Lonely Planet*. Study your guidebook well before you arrive. Don't worry about not knowing the language. Use a language app; memorize key phrases like "Thank you," "Please," and "Where is the bathroom?" Pack light (small suitcase or backpack), and plan to wash clothes as you go. Use the internet before and during your domestic or your foreign trip. Google "travel on the cheap."

Places to Stay

With Airbnb.com, set up an account. I recommend you stay in a home where you can interact with your host family.

You can also go couch surfing. Members pay an annual fee twenty-two to sixty-four dollars if you are not a host. Often, you can have a spare room rather than the couch.

With Workaway.info, agree to work a few hours a day, and you stay for free in a dedicated part of the facility. It's not for everyone, but what an experience. Some provide food. Check it out.

Trivago.com, Priceline.com, Bookings.com, Travelocity.com, and many more online sites compare room prices. Do your research and identify the site that works best for you. Keep your eyes open. When I last checked in to my Bookings.com motel, the lady in front of me received a lower price. I asked, actually insisted, on the lower price. And got it.

Tours

Check out Intrepid Travel. I generally avoid tours where you have to stay with the group the entire trip. Intrepid Travel is an exception. Tours are small (twelve or so max); there are a few scheduled meals, but most are on your own. Each trip includes a project to benefit the destination country.

Gate 1 Travel was recommended by a friend. Gate 1 offers escorted tours, European river cruises, independent vacations, and customized international vacation packages for less.

Tripsavvy.com provides guides to the world's best destinations, tricks for booking hotel rooms, and tips for finding the best things to do wherever you go.

Check a travel agency. I haven't used one in decades, but one or two should be part of the mix.

Food

To save money, eat at your hotel if breakfast is provided, and eat big. If breakfast is not included, bring along a small immersion heater to make hot water (first, make sure the local water is drinkable). The hot water is perfect for oatmeal and coffee. Make your own lunches from items at the grocery store—ham, cheese, bread,

MONEY SENSE FOR YOUNG PROFESSIONALS

yogurt, and drinks. Check your guidebook for reasonably priced dinners. If you need to drink water, buy it at the supermarket or kiosk. It will cost three times more if you sit down at a café. Eat not with other tourists. Eat where the locals eat. It will be cheaper and much more interesting. If facilities are available at your hotel, cook your own meals.

Transportation Abroad

Check out the trains. Best way to travel in Europe and much of the world is by train. Stations are near the city center, and some have tourist information and provide booking assistance.

Study the local transportation. Learn how the buses and trams work. Many cities/countries offer passes good on all forms of transit for one day or more.

Airlines

Google.com/flights—I start here to find which airlines go where, when, and the pricing. Once I have selected the specific flight, I follow up (on another browser) with the airline website first. I often follow through and start the booking process through Google.

Kayak.com is another often recommended starting point. Many others are available.

It is not as much fun or convenient to fly now as it was decades ago. I dislike deep discount airlines that don't let you get a boarding pass ahead of time, sell you a seat for an additional fee, charge extra for luggage (I tire of explaining to TSA why I am wearing five sets of underwear), and charge for water. Avoid United's basic economy. I was so outraged with the service that I wrote the CEO a letter. I told him if the airline wanted more money, it should serve coffee in larger cups and then charge for the use of the airplane's bathroom. The reply letter said they are passing my suggestion to the committee!

Discounts

Ultimate Guide to Travel Discounts (2019) (https://tinyurl. com/y35nwsdp).

Check travel rewards programs.

Apply for memberships. Often you can get discounts if you belong to various organizations. Have your membership cards available. And if you have ever served, tell them you are a veteran. Whenever priority boarding is announced, I tell the gate person I am a veteran and ask if that is priority. It works sometimes. Once, the representative said that it is not corporate policy but personally "go ahead and board."

Language and Customs

Your goal may be to see the sites as a tourist. But travel investment is best spent meeting the locals and learning the culture.

Mark Twain said, "Travel is fatal to prejudice, bigotry and narrow-mindedness, and many of our people need it" (1869 and still very relevant today).

Travel Tips

Traveling is enjoyable, but spend a lot of time planning before you leave:

☐ **Prepare**. Get a haircut. You want your hair short and manageable. You will need a good hat, sunglasses, and an extra pair of regular glasses. Take your medications. Bring along a smallish and easy-to-use camera. Take a notebook to jot down impressions. Make sure your passport is up to date. Learn the currency and how to move around (train, bus, walking) in each country/city you are visiting. Study the travel guide, and check for discounts and fun things to do that don't cost too much. Make sure the souvenirs are made in the country you are visiting. Learn a few words of the local language, and if you have food allergies, know how to voice them. Take small gifts for homestays and cloth bracelets for the kids. Remember to take along a lot of patience and a good sense of humor.

☐ **Clothing**. Wear casual, lightweight clothing, which is easy to wash and quick to dry. My travel shirt has a deep, zippered inside pocket to protect daily spending money. It is a good idea to keep most of your money and your passport in a money belt. My pants can easily be turned into shorts by unzipping the trouser legs. For the ladies, pack similar outfits, including a dress for all occasions. There is no need for different or fancy clothes. Do not carry a purse; use a vest or pocked shirt instead. Leave expensive jewelry at home; take one necklace and one pair of earrings that go with everything. My travel vest, which has too many zippered compartments to count, holds all pocket items so when I go through airport security, I just take off the vest and put it on the tray.

☐ **Packing**. Take a suitcase that is small, easy to transport, and fits in the overhead compartment on the airplane. You will spend much time walking with your luggage both in the airport and in each city. It should be lockable.

☐ **Foreign money.** Converting to foreign money is always a challenge. Understand the exchange rate so you can compute the value of each intended purchase. You want to get the best rate. You don't want to carry too much, and you don't want to have to convert money back into dollars at the end of the trip. I no longer exchange money in the States before I leave because the exchange rate tends to be very bad. For initial arrival expenses, I change a modest amount at the arriving airport. Once established, I find the best exchange rates in town. Bring a credit card that has no foreign exchange fees, and use it whenever possible. A credit card transaction most often has the best exchange rate, and with no transaction fees, it is a good way to conserve your foreign currency.

Prior planning prevents poor performance. Plan ahead and have a great trip!

Planning Self-Travel: The Top Five

If you or the family are traveling alone, concentrate pretravel planning on these five areas. Use your travel guide (I use *Lonely Planet*) and the internet.

1. **Money.** Understand the various exchange rates: your bank before you go (worst rate; only exchange a small amount); in the destination country's bank rate(s) (good rate; avoid large airport exchange); your credit card, which has no exchange fee (best rate). Once you exchange in the destination country, write down various exchanges for the rate you received (example: 20 Brazilian reals = $5.22, 100 = $26, etc.)

2. **Transportation.** Figure out the most practical way to travel within a city (transportation pass) and between cities (train). Many cities have passes to all forms of local transport (bus, tram, subway) for a number of days. Trains are the best way to travel between cities and countries in many places. They take you from town center to town center, where further connections and assistance are available.

3. **Accommodations.** I usually reserve a hotel for one or two nights in my destination city and then use the guidebook to find hotels in other cities after I arrive. Airbnb is good, especially if you stay in a room and share facilities with your host family. Reservations recommended. Stay where the locals stay, and avoid tourist hotels, where the experience is no different than at home. If you know someone abroad, ask if they will host you during your trip. I recommend flexibility rather than planning every overnight in advance.

4. **Food.** Get off the beaten path, and enjoy the local cuisine. Many menus have pictures. If you have no idea what you are ordering, figure out where the entrées are on the menu and point to one. Travel is an adventure; eat different.

5. **What to see.** Determine ahead of time what you "must" see. Purchase tickets online to avoid the ticket lines. Best is to walk around nontouristed areas and absorb the culture. Try not to look like a tourist.

CHAPTER 13

Retirement

Saving for Retirement

Borrow Money from My 401(k)? Not!

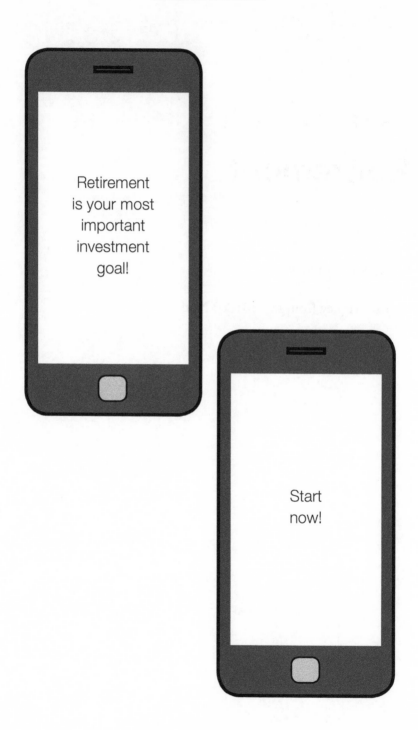

Saving for Retirement

Wait, wait! Don't skip this important part!

You may be a young professional, but that does not mean you should not think about your future, even your far distant future. Consider this: each day you work now must pay for today and for some day in the future when you will not be earning an income, when you are retired. Remember too that over the decades, changes in retirement accounts are inevitable.

If Social Security is still around, monthly Social Security direct deposits into your bank account may provide funds to live on. But Social Security is designed only to provide some money, maybe 40% of what you will actually need. You must supplement this income with other savings. While working, your contribution to Social Security is taken out of your paycheck before you receive your pay. Since 1983, Social Security has slowly reduced the exhaustion date from 2058 to 2034, and a report from the University of Pennsylvania Warton School of Business lists 2032 as the end date. The government probably will make some changes prior. Bottom line: don't count on Social Security. Also, don't count on an inheritance.

If you work for the federal or state government, the education or health sectors, or some large corporations and stay with them for a designated number of years, you may qualify for a pension. But overall, pensions are becoming history.

A 401(k) plan (or equivalent) is an employer-sponsored retirement plan. You have the option to place a percentage of your gross pay in an investment account. This money is pretax. You don't pay taxes on this income in the year invested. You pay taxes when you take it out decades in the future. Also, the growth of this invested money is not taxed until taken out. Most often, your employer also contributes a percentage to your plan. This is called "free money" and is one of the biggest perks of working for your employer. I recommend you contribute as much as your plan allows, but make sure you put in enough to get the maximum employer match. Check with HR.

In addition to Social Security and 401(k), you also can open an IRA (individual retirement account). You may contribute up to $6,000 per year (2019) in an IRA account as long as you have what is called earned income. This maximum increases to $7,000 when you reach age fifty. A nonworking spouse also can open an IRA, as long as the amount of money both spouses contribute is "earned income." You open an IRA yourself and then determine the mix of investments. Remember, do not invest in anything recommended by a financial person who receives a commission on the purchase. They are working on their retirement, not yours.

An IRA also can be a Roth IRA. The difference is the Roth is aftertax money, while the regular IRA is pretax money. The benefit of the Roth is huge, and a Roth is highly recommended. Because you already paid taxes on the Roth contribution, the contributed money is not taxed when you take in out in retirement. And the growth (capital gains) of that money also is never taxed. In a regular IRA, both the contributions and the growth of the contributions are taxed as "income" when taken out. The growth in an IRA account can be huge since it will not be used for decades. There now are Roth 401(k) accounts also. Check with HR to see if this option is offered.

Once your money is in a retirement account, leave it there, and do not take it out. Withdrawal from a regular IRA or 401(k) account before age fifty-nine and a half adds a 10% penalty to the taxes. Withdrawal of the money contributed to a Roth account is not taxed if withdrawn early, but don't do it.

You can supplement your "retirement" investments with regular nonretirement investments. Advantages: more money to live on during retirement (think bucket list), no withdrawal penalty if needed prior, and the growth of your investments are taxed at the lower "capital gains" rate.

Put aside money for retirement when you get your first full-time job.

Borrow Money from My 401(k)? Not!

One in seven workers will borrow money from the 401(k) company retirement plan. Is this a good idea or not? It is a simple as one, two, three.

1. If you pay off debt with a windfall of cash without solving the problem that got you into debt in the first place, you will be in worse financial shape within two years. A 401(k) loan would be considered a windfall of cash.
2. If you do not have positive cash flow, you have two choices: make more or spend less. Borrowing money to cover the difference is not an option.
3. The most important reason to save is your retirement.

I do not recommend taking a loan from your 401(k). There are features that make the loan seem attractive: low interest rate, no credit check, and you pay interest to yourself. In fact, back when I was in my thirties, I did take out a 401(k) loan to buy a car. I figured, what could be better than paying interest to myself? It was years later that I learned the facts. Your 401(k) money is pretax; you pay taxes when you take it out. The interest you pay on a 401(k) loan goes back into your retirement plan. The problem is that the interest you pay has already been taxed, and it will be taxed a second time when you withdraw the money. Paying tax twice is just not very smart.

Messing with money set aside for retirement is not a good plan. You will need this money in the years ahead. And if you lose your job, you only have sixty days to repay the loan. If you can't pay the money back and you are under fifty-nine and a half, the amount is taxed, and a 10% penalty is assessed.

Most of the time, taking a loan from your 401(k) will put you on the road to financial disaster.

CHAPTER 14

Hints

Treat Your Money Like You Treat Your Car

Teens Prepare for the Real Money World

Use a Year-by-Year Chart

How to Prepare a Net Worth Statement

Be Careful When Starting a Side Business

It's the Little Things

Treat Your Money Like You Treat Your Car

How is your car like your money? When you have a new car (or a car that's new to you), you are proud of your car, and you take care of your car. When figuring out who is responsible for your car, you don't look at TV ads or social media to find someone to take over responsibility for your car. You accept that responsibility, because it's your car. You should do the same thing for your money. It's your money; take responsibility.

Take care of your car, and it will take care of you. You pay attention to your car. You put gas in, you wash it, you protect it with insurance, and you protect it by parking in the far corners of the lot where someone cannot open a door into it. Your money needs attention also. And it needs protection.

Your car needs a new windshield. So you take it to someone qualified to install windshields. You don't want someone trained to sell windshields; you don't want someone whose boss has placed a quota of selling and installing twenty-five windshields a day. When your money needs some fixing, take it to someone with your best interests at heart; don't take it to someone with a quota for selling you something.

If you loan your car to someone, you expect him or her to bring it back—and bring it back with a full tank of gas. Now you know how a bank feels when they loan money on your credit card. They want their money back, just like you want your car back. Think about this when you contemplate missing a credit card payment.

Some people think finances and investing are difficult; they think they cannot possibly learn about finances. Think about owning and driving and maintaining your car. You had to learn how to operate and take care of a car. You can learn how to take care of your money. All it takes is a little dedication and a lot of common sense.

The point is, treat your money better. Spend more time taking care of your money.

You love your car, so start loving your money!

Teens Prepare for the Real Money World

Teens answer questions about money. Learn from them and the Money Coach's comments.

1. **Michael, age sixteen**
   Question: What have you done right with your money?
   MICHAEL. I created a checking and savings account.
   MONEY COACH. Good job, especially on the savings account. Make sure you keep track of your balance, and never write a check when there is not enough money to cover it.
   MICHAEL. When I got my first job, I started depositing 20% of each paycheck into my savings account.
   MONEY COACH. Very good. You started at the very beginning of your earning life. Keep saving money.
   MICHAEL. I only ask someone for money if I know I can pay them back.
   MONEY COACH. This is a life lesson. You borrow money; you must be in a position to pay it back.

   Question: What do you want to know about money?
   MICHAEL. Is it no credit at all, zero credit, when you first get your credit card at eighteen?
   MONEY COACH. You are more likely to be classified as "no credit history" rather than "credit score zero." Before you even think about a credit card, know well that you must be in a position to pay the entire bill at month's end. That means you must track your purchases so you won't overspend. Never place yourself in a position where you must pay interest because you can't pay the entire bill.

MONEY SENSE FOR YOUNG PROFESSIONALS

MICHAEL. Is it better to get a credit card under your parents or alone?

MONEY COACH. As you reach your late teens and early twenties, I recommend you start your own money life, a life without your parents. Stand on your own!

MICHAEL. Is the best way to establish credit through a prepaid card?

MONEY COACH. What you want is a "secured" card, which is an actual credit card that reports to the credit bureaus. A prepaid card is like a gift card or a debit card and does not help establish a credit history. Check with your bank or credit union. You also may be able to open an account with, for example, $400 and then borrow that amount as a personal loan and pay it back with the deposit. Remember to consider interest. Again, check with your banking institution. The biggest portion of your credit score is whether you pay your bills on time. Start early paying bills in your name: cell phone, car payment, car insurance, utilities, rent, etc. Check your credit score for free at CreditKarma.com.

2. **Sarah, age seventeen**
Question: What have you done right with your money?

SARAH. Mother has started a college savings account.

MONEY COACH. Good. Remember that paying for college is a joint effort of student, parents, grandparents, friends. "Skin in the game" means being involved in reaching a goal. If the student has made no financial contribution in paying for college, the parents' money might be considered a Budweiser scholarship.

SARAH. I am saving all spare change, including pennies.

189

MONEY COACH. Yes, save the change, but also start saving bills. Start small. One dollar a week for month one, two dollars a week month two, etc.

SARAH. I will get a secured credit card when able to.

MONEY COACH. Always be cautious when using a credit card.

Question: What do you want to know about money?

SARAH. What is the best type of fixed-rate mortgage?

MONEY COACH. Mortgages are complicated. Long before purchasing a house, explore the world of mortgages. Interview many real estate and mortgage people. Best, of course, is lowest rate. Determine how much house you are able to buy, and then find the mortgage that best fits your financial status. Put enough money down so you do not have to pay mortgage insurance.

SARAH. Is it better to have a low fixed rate over a thirty-year period or a higher fixed rate over a shorter period?

MONEY COACH. We currently [2019] are in a period where interest rates are moving higher, so a fixed rate is best. The real answer is what can you afford. Personally, I would rather have the longest time period possible because the payments will be lower. You can always sell and pay off the balance. Be careful when considering extra payments to principal on your mortgage. While you will reduce the length of the mortgage slightly (thirty years first becomes twenty-nine and a half years), the monthly payment will stay the same until you reach the end date or sell the house.

SARAH. Does your credit score affect the time you have to pay back a mortgage?

MONEY COACH. No, your mortgage will have a set time no matter your score. The credit score affects the interest rate. The higher the score, generally the lower the rate. Work hard on establishing a good (720 or higher) score before buying a house.

Ask yourself these questions frequently.

Use a Year-by-Year Chart

To help plan your money life, make and use a year-by-year chart. Start with a blank piece of paper (or an Excel spreadsheet). Draw three vertical lines top to bottom from the left each, three-fourths an inch apart. Label the first column "Year"; the second column, "My age"; the third column, "Spouse's age." The next column should be four inches wide; label this "Significant events that affect my money." The last column is "Money, where to, where from."

Fill in the date and age all the way down the sheet. Then under "Significant event," project identifiable and noteworthy money events that will happen in your life (see below) and draw a horizontal line under that year. Determine if the event will bring money in or money out of your budget. Then determine where that money will go or where it will come from.

Here are some events to consider:

- Pay off student debt. (What is the goal of the "new" money now that you are finished, finally, with student debt as an expenditure?)
- Next year, start a new career. (Budget how much for savings, how much for retirement.)
- Buy a car or buy a house. (Which account will fund the new car or new house?)
- Christmas next year. (Budget how much; start putting money aside now.)
- Kids out of day care and into school. (Into which account will this saved money go? And for what purpose?)
- Trip to Africa in three years, $3,000. (Better start saving $100 a month now.)
- Year kids will be teenagers (buy earplugs), when they will go to college (how to pay), when they will leave the household (room available to rent).
- House paid off.
- Early retirement.
- Begin Social Security.

What you have is your entire life laid out on the front and back of one sheet of paper. Use the chart as a planning tool. You will be surprised how useful this might be. Things happen, so revisit/redraw your chart every couple of years.

Remember the five *P*s: prior planning prevents poor performance.

Year	Wife's age	Husband's age	Significant life or money event	Money from where or money to where
2019	30	29	son born	college fund, add to budget
2020	31	30	-	-
2021	32	31	-	-
2022	33	32	-	-
2023	34	33	-	-
2024	35	34	buy home	from down payment bucket

How to Prepare a Net Worth Statement

A net worth statement is how much money you are worth right now; it is the cash value of everything you own (assets) minus how much money you owe (liabilities). I recommend everyone do a net worth statement once a year, and the first week of January is a good time to start.

All you need is a pencil and paper and your financial records. You can then put the data on an Excel spreadsheet, which does the math for you.

On the left-hand side of the page, put down all your assets: cash, investments, retirement accounts, real estate, household contents, automobiles, value of business interests, and anything else you own that has monetary value. If someone owes you money, put it down as an asset. If you have a stamp collection, put down your estimated value of the collection. The goal is to write down the value of everything you own.

On the right-hand side, list everything you owe, your liabilities: mortgage, car loan, credit card debt (only if you carry a balance), student loans, personal loans, and any other money you owe anyone.

Add the total assets, and subtract the total liabilities, and you have your net worth.

A big caution here. The net worth figure does not represent the amount of money you will walk away with if you cash in everything. The amount realized from the sale of your home will be less because you have to pay a commission on the sale. You probably overvalued the cash price of your automobile. Investment accounts contain capital gains, which will be taxed. The money in retirement accounts (except Roth accounts) will be taxed as income when taken out. Your household contents will be of more value to you than to someone else.

The goal of this exercise is to establish a baseline value net worth at a point in time. Then compare this year's net worth to your net worth at the same time next year and every year thereafter. This is a great way to monitor your overall financial progress!

Be Careful When Starting a Side Business

Brad didn't have a clue on how to handle the money he made as a DJ on weekends. The cash just went into his pocket and was used for whatever expenditure came next, business related or not. When Brad came to see me, his Money Coach, I had him follow these five steps to run a successful business:

- **Step 1.** Any business involves planning, and any business, no matter how small in scope or income, should have a thoughtful, written business plan.
- **Step 2.** Separate your business money from your family money. Set up a business structure according to your personal needs: sole proprietorship (use your name for the business, like John Smith Plumbing, or register a trade name, like Plumbing Done Right), LLC (limited liability company), S corporation, or C corporation. Seek the advice of accounting, financial, and legal experts. The goal is to set up a separate entity to deal with business issues and business finances.
- **Step 3.** Make sure you track all business expenses separately from the family budget.
- **Step 4.** Determine how much, if any, your side business needs to contribute to the family budget. If your day job covers family expenses, then determine what will be done with the business money left over after business expenses are paid.
- **Step 5.** Determine the company profit. Keep careful records, information useful to you but also information that can be used by outside sources, such as an accountant or the IRS. Profit can be used to build the business, or it can be used for other purposes. The idea is to know what the money will be used for. There are many wonderful ways to build a nest egg for retirement with profits from your side business. If there are no profits, then you must ask yourself if it is a real busi-

ness or just a hobby. The IRS frowns on taxpayers who list the costs of a hobby as business losses. Be careful.

We all have some entrepreneurial spirit within us. With a little planning, a side business can be educational and profitable.

MONEY SENSE FOR YOUNG PROFESSIONALS

It's the Little Things

Many of us have problems with our money because we think all financial stuff is complicated and difficult or impossible to understand. In reality, it's the little things that matter!

Pick up that penny. Too often, young people walk past a penny on the pavement. A penny is money. You must respect money. You must care about money, especially wasting it. Develop a positive attitude about money, even that penny. Your job today is to save that penny from the street. Pick up that penny. That penny's job is to make your day.

Save the shower water while it is warming up; use it to water your vegetable garden.

Take twenty pounds out the trunk to save gas. Check your tire pressure.

Avoid ATM and bank fees.

Send ecards; they are free, and people love them.

Use a debit card instead of a credit card.

Buy generic; eat out less. Drink the coffee at work. Figure out how much a $3.50 Starbucks coffee will set you back over a lifetime.

I remember a coworker whose mother had a box labeled "Pieces of string too short to keep." Older generations seem more frugal. Many young people could use a dose of frugalness.

Go to restaurants where there is free parking.

Get movies and books at the library.

Combine errands; walk or bike more often.

Before you shop anywhere, search for coupons online for that store.

Go one week longer before the next haircut.

Beware automatic renewal of memberships and magazines.

The big thing to remember is, it's your attitude toward money that matters!

RESOURCES

Resources from the Money Coach, the Author

Money Coach Bill's website, MoneyCoachBill.org, with articles across twelve categories (https://tinyurl.com/yd78agqb).

Bill Stanley's Facebook page, with notifications of new articles, short money sense tips, links to subjects of interest (https://tinyurl.com/ychfafk2).

Money Sense for Young Professionals' Facebook page, (https://tinyurl.com/y6l4mbls).

Bill Stanley's LinkedIn, a repository for recent Money Coach articles (https://tinyurl.com/y9owftzs).

Bill Stanley's Chirp, with short less-than-a-minute audios with money sense tips (https://tinyurl.com/ycyx34cr).

Zorro the Money Dog (a real dog) talks to preschool and elementary school kids via one-minute videos that include a parent/teacher guide for each episode (https://tinyurl.com/j5my2rb).

Resources: Books

Designing Your Life, book by Bill Burnett and Dave Evans. Learn how to figure out your career path (https://tinyurl.com/y9ogkmck).

Way of the Warrior Kid: From Wimpy to Warrior the Navy SEAL Way, book by Jocko Willink. It contains lessons from a fifth grader and his Navy SEAL uncle (https://tinyurl.com/y88aw69z).

Richest Man in Babylon, written in 1926 by George Clason. It covers money basics learned a long time ago; the lessons are still valuable today (https://tinyurl.com/zvfhfb8).

Who Owns the Ice House? Eight Life Lessons from an Unlikely Entrepreneur, by Gary Schoeniger and Clifton Taulbert. Learn life's financial lessons from an unlikely entrepreneur (https://tinyurl.com/ydf3hr79).

Resources for Purchasing an Automobile (From PikesPeakontheCheap.com)

AutoTrader.com. The app lets you search for new, used, and certified pre-owned cars near you via GPS or by a particular type of engine or transmission, such as an eco-boost engine or a six-speed with a sport shift. Neat feature: you can scan the VIN (vehicle identification number) barcode on a vehicle whose history of ownership you'd like to find, or you can scan for a similar one nearby.

Cars.com. Look for new and used cars for sale in your area, read reviews, and calculate estimated car payments. Using their On the Lot tool, and you can compare inventory between dealers. Neat feature: find certified repair centers to have your car serviced, and research fair prices to pay for repairs.

CARFAX. Once you sign up for an account at CarFax.com, you can run a vehicle history report on the car you are interested in buying. Scan the VIN bar code or manually type in the seventeen-digit number. Neat feature: type in the vehicle license plate for a search to make sure the plate matches the vehicle.

Consumer Reports. Consumer Reports offers an app that is a guidebook on buying a used car. You can look at car ratings and calculate loan or lease payments. Neat feature: Ask the Right Questions category gives you sample questions to ask a seller once you have found a car you like.

Edmunds.com. This car guru has long been a go-to for car buyers. The app lets you search pricing and inventory at dealerships close to home. There's also a calculator to help you calculate monthly loan or lease payments. Neat feature: get Edmund's "true market value" to see what a particular model is selling for in your geographic region, and locate a dealer within a specific distance who is offering an incentive deal.

Honcker.com. Honcker lets you check prices and calculate your monthly rate on leased cars in your area. If you find a car within a twenty-five-mile radius of your location, you can have the car delivered to you free. Neat feature: Honcker runs a soft credit check. Lease transactions can be done within hours, with quick application processes.

KBB.com, also known as Kelley Blue Book. The app lets you search by manufacturer for new cars and by year for used ones and includes reviews by both professional automotive journalists and consumers who own or lease the model. Neat feature: there are videos for vehicles that interest you, plus some you could afford, like the 2013 Dodge Viper.

TrueCar.com. Search for a used or new car, and receive a price calculated by what others have paid for the same car. It's easy to navigate, and more than twelve thousand dealers participate. Neat feature: TrueCar scans window stickers at dealerships that are included in their database so you can get a fair market price in your area.

Used Car Search Pro, iSeeCars. This app allows you to view millions of used cars and trucks for sale by owners and dealers across the country. Narrow down the search by using a number of search filters, including price, third-row seats, and even the amount of headroom in the cab. The cars are also listed according to best price, above and below market prices. Neat feature: email alerts tell you if a saved vehicle price has changed.

Resources for Paying for Higher Education

Official Money Guide for College Students—a book (https://tinyurl.com/ycgn4w3y).

Summary of VA Educational Benefits—pdf download (https://tinyurl.com/ya2zhcam).

FAFSA (Free Application for Federal Student Aid)—articles (https://tinyurl.com/nr2amqb).

Scholly—an app; find scholarships, Apple products, $2.99/month (https://tinyurl.com/y8bz6bxd).

"A Beginner's Guide to Repaying Student Loans"—an article (https://tinyurl.com/ydc85j4u).

"Student Debt Repayment"—*USAA Magazine* article summary (https://tinyurl.com/yafd8s6b).

Maine Tax Incentive Program—your annual student loan is credited to your state income tax (https://tinyurl.com/y8tuo4uu).

Employers helping pay student loans—article (https://tinyurl.com/ydea3gkf).

Free On-Line Courses—MOOCs, or Massive Open Online Courses (https://tinyurl.com/y7ygarux).

ABOUT THE AUTHOR

Bill Stanley has been a Registered Investment Adviser since 2001. He is not your traditional financial adviser. Instead of selling financial products and taking control of peoples' money, Bill is a coach, a Money Coach. His overall mission as a Money Coach is to help everyone with their money. His beloved dog, Zorro, does one-minute videos for elementary school children—google "Zorro the Money Dog." Bill works with high schoolers with presentations such as "Ten Things Teens Need to Know About Money" in coordination with the nonprofit organization Peak Education. His audiences range from third graders (Junior Achievement) to retirees (Senior Center). Bill volunteers his time with numerous organizations and nonprofits. For over ten years Bill was the Money Matters guy on *Fox 21 Morning News* with more than three hundred live appearances before the Colorado Springs TV audience.

Money Coach is Bill's Sixth career. His previous careers: U.S. Marine, diplomat (Africa), program manager at a high tech company, advertising sales associate for several publications, photographer. Number seven is author.

Bill believes the best investment is education, and the best education can come from foreign travel where you can observe and participate in other cultures. Bill has traveled widely, all 50 states and 75 countries (and counting). He has lived overseas for six years, the military (Vietnam, the Caribbean, and Guantanamo Bay, Cuba) and the Diplomatic Corps (four years with our embassies in Ghana and Kenya). Bill shares travel advice in the Travel chapter.

Bill and Zorro live in Colorado Springs, Colorado.

Money Coach Bill's passions and goals have merged:

> #1—help as many people as he can in matters of money and life
>
> #2—travel/travel/travel